I LIVE MY DREAMS IN 3-D

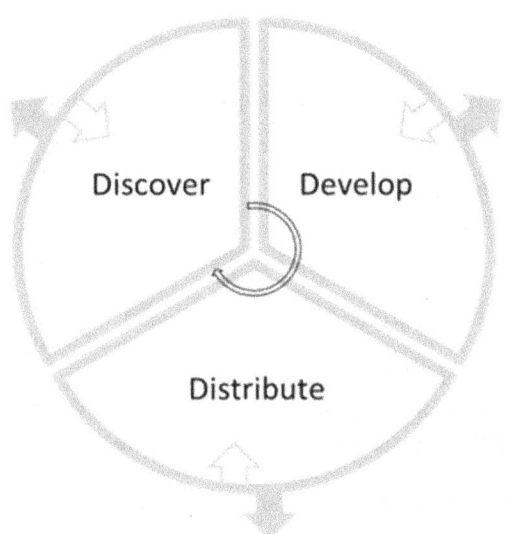

BRIAN M. JONES

I Live My Dreams In 3-D: Discover, Develop, and Distribute Your Dreams to the World.

Jones, Brian M. (1977-)

Entrepreneurship, coaching, business, self-development

TM & © 2013. Brian M. Jones. All rights reserved.

No part of this work may be reproduced in any form, or by any means whatsoever, without written permission from the author, except in the case of brief quotations embodied in critical articles and reviews.

Published in Philadelphia, Pennsylvania, USA. December 2013.

This publication contains the opinions and ideas of its author. It is meant to strengthen your common sense, not to substitute for it. It is also not a substitute for the advice of your doctor, lawyer, accountant, or any of your advisors, personal or professional.

Welcome to
I LIVE MY DREAMS IN 3-D
Discover, Develop, and Distribrute Your Dreams to the World™

[Dreams] deferred makes the heart sick, but a [dream] fulfilled is a tree of life. – Bible, Proverbs 13:12 (modified)

Congratulations for taking steps to make your dream a reality!

A "dreamer" is often viewed as a person who has many ideas but never seems to live out those ideas in the "real world." This does not have to be your existence.

In the context of Dream In 3-D, a dreamer is a person who gets clear on a goal, creates a way to achieve the goal, and invites others to support along the way.

As you grow accustomed to the habits of discovering your purpose, developing your paths, and distributing (your dreams) through people, you will conceive and complete your dreams in more consistent and automatic fashion. Finishing what you fathom will be a natural way of life. You will then inspire others to do the same.

In this book, I share about the *Evolution of a Dream* - the process of bringing your dreams into being, and the *Evolution of the Dreamer* - the perspectives that help you maintain your balance as your pursue your dreams.

While there are no easy steps for achieving your dreams, "I Live My Dreams In 3-D"offers principles and practices that will improve your rate of success.

I wish you the best in your pursuit of dreams that profit you, your family, your friends, and fellow-citizens of the global community.

Brian M. Jones
Philadelphia, PA, 2013

Table of
CONTENTS

The Evolution of a Dream	5
Process 1: Discover My Purpose	11
Process 2: Develop My Paths	44
Process 3: Distribute Through People	60
The Evolution of a Dreamer	71
Perspective 1: Peace	75
Perspective 2: Flow	80
Perspective 3: Pace	84
A Final Thought: Dream. Reality. Same Thing.	88

Introduction
THE EVOLUTION OF A DREAM

The Evolution of a Dream is the process by which you transform your dream from a mental concept into a concrete reality.

This evolution occurs through the continual process of discovery, development, and distribution. Your objective is to be aware of, and influence, these phases of evolution as much as possible in order to improve your chances of successfully fulfilling your dream.

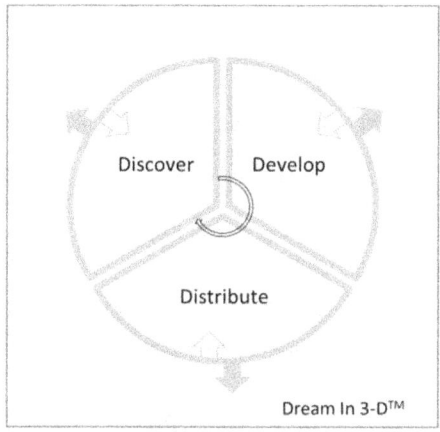

Discover My Purpose: What are my desired facts of life?

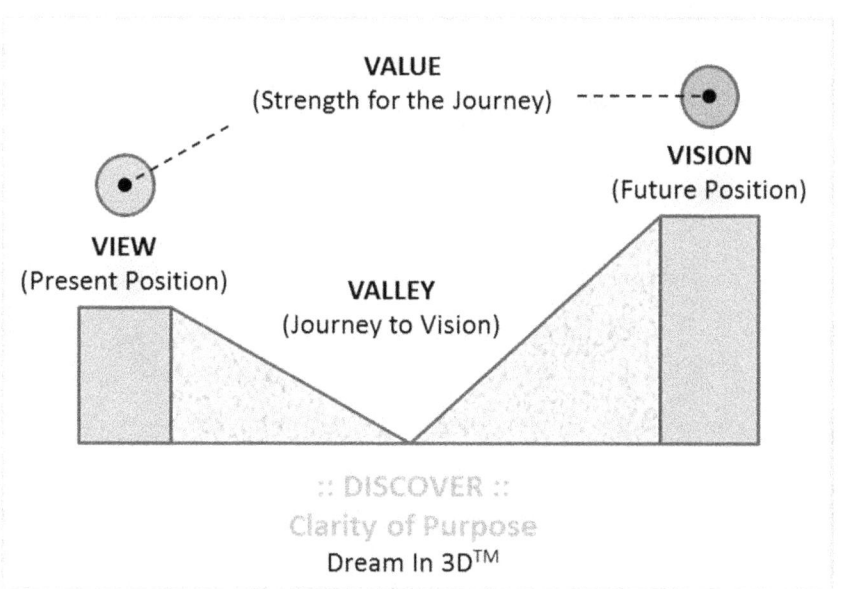

Discovery is the first step in the "I Live My Dreams In 3-D" process. The goal of discovery is for you to have clarity about your purpose. You will know that you have clarity of purpose when you can clearly identify, picture, and articulate your:

- **Vision** - a vivid picture of what you want for your life (your future position);
- **View** - an honest description of your present circumstances (your present position);
- **Valley** - a realistic understanding of the gap that exists between your vision and your view (your journey); and
- **Value** – the strengths you possess, the resources you can acess, and how you will apply them towards achieving your dreams (the strength for your journey).

The clearer the picture you have about your life, the better chance you will have of producing your desired reality.

Develop My Paths: What steps will I take to achieve my desired facts of life?

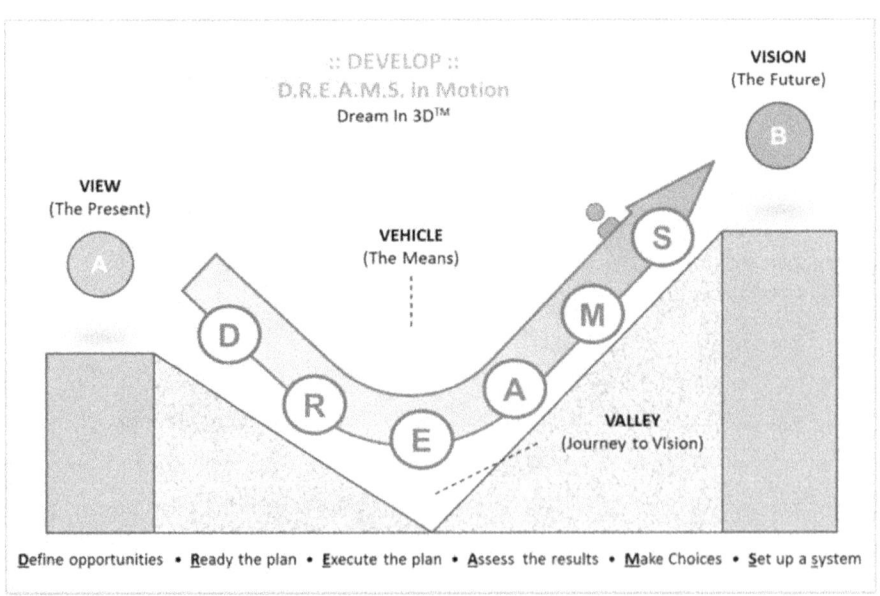

Development is the second step in the "I Live My Dreams In 3-D" process. The goal of development is for you to plan, and execute, a specific course of action for achieving your dream. Development is not just a set of tasks to complete; it is a set of habits you repeat:

- **Define opportunities** - identify and evaluate options for pursuing, and achieving, a given goal;
- **Ready your plan** - outline a step-by-step plan for maximizing a selected opportunity;
- **Execute your plan** - complete the steps that you outlined;
- **Assess your results** - evaluate what you accomplished;
- **Make choices** - based upon results, decide to stick with what you are doing or take a different approach; and
- **Set up a system** - identify your best opportunities and steps; make them part of your regular routine.

Success is certain when you consistently follow-through on wisely-selected opportunities.

Distribute Through People: Who is championing my dream?

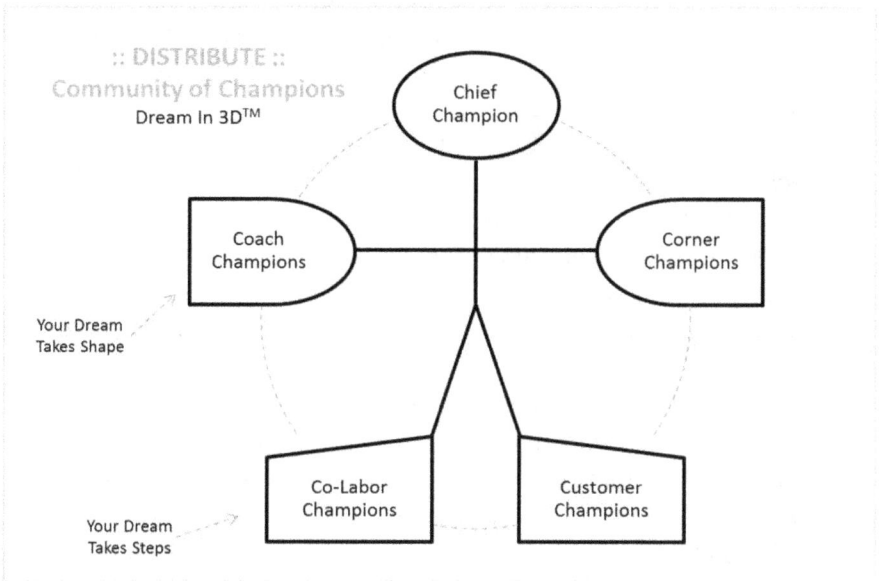

Distribution is the third step in the "I Live My Dreams In 3-D" process. The goal of distribution is to recruit a team of people who will help you champion your dream These champions will help you achieve your dream as if it were their own:

- **Chief Champion** - the person most responsible for fulfilling the dream (you);
- **Corner Champions** - loved ones who are "in your corner" and support you personally as you pursue your dreams;
- **Coach Champions** - experienced role-models who offer trusted advice;
- **Co-Labor Champions** - skilled contributors who assist you with executing your plans; and
- **Consumer Champions** - people who benefit from, and value, your fulfilled dream.

You achieve lasting success when you: (a) develop a community of champtions who support your dreams, and (b) faithfully champion the dreams of others.

My Dream Evolution Profile

This is a great time to consider your own approach to pursuing dreams. Use the survey below as a guide to reflect upon your typical approach to pursuing your dreams.

Read each statement.
- ☑ Place a check next to each statement that you do well.
- ☒ Place an "x" next to each statement that you do sometimes but know you need to improve.
- ☐ Leave a statement blank if it is an item that you do not do at present.

Category 1: Discover My Purpose
- ☐ I know what facts I want to be true about each area of my life.
- ☐ I face the current facts of my life as a start on dreams. I deal with my current reality.
- ☐ I know my strengths and I apply them all towards the pursuit of my dreams.

> Category 2: Develop My Paths
> - ☐ I prioritize & schedule time to fully develop and complete my dreams.
> - ☐ I prepare a specific, detailed plan of action for each dream.
> - ☐ I follow-through on each step of my action plan.
>
> Category 3: Distribute Through People
> - ☐ I invest more into my dream than I request from others. I lead the way.
> - ☐ I form relationships with others where we both win as a result of working together.
> - ☐ I invite others to help me complete my dream.
>
> # of checks (☑) _____   # of x's (☒) _____   # of blanks (☐) _____

This survey helps you confirm steps that you favor as well as parts of the process that you tend to skip. The purpose of this guide is for you to improve how you complete of all aspects of the "I Live My Dreams In 3-D" process so that you accomplish your goals with a greater level of success.

Next Steps
1. Review key concepts from this section: Discover, Develop, Distribute
2. Review the Dream Evolution Profile results. Share your results with family, friends, and others you trust for feedback.
3. Reflect on the following:
   - What did you learn about yourself as a result of the profiler?

   _____

   _____

   - How close were your answers aligned with how you are viewed by others?

   _____

   _____

   - In what ways are you happy with your approach to pursuing dreams?

- In what ways do you plan to improve your approach pursuing dreams?

4. Identify 1 dream you have in mind. What is the current status of your dream *(e.g. not started, in-progress, almost done)*? How close are you to the dream becoming your reality? What "I Live My Dreams In 3-D" step(s) will you take <u>right now</u> to improve your progress? (Use a separate sheet if needed)

Process 1
DISCOVER MY PURPOSE

Achieving your dreams begins with having a clear mental picture of what you want. **Discover My Purpose** is the process by which you will paint that picture upon the canvas of your mind. The more that picture becomes engrained in your mind, the more you will begin to live as if it is real. The way you think and behave in reality will increasingly match your mental picture. If you see yourself running a business, you will take on those habits. If you see yourself being disciplined with diet and fitness, you will take on those habits. In doing so, you will begin to build momentum towards your vision becoming your reality.

Vision. View. Valley. Value.
During the process of discovery, you will identify your vision, view, valley, and value. Your vision is your ideal future position – i.e. the goal you wish to reach. Your view is your present position – i.e. your current progress as it relates to your goal. Your valley is the distance that exists between your vision (future position) and your view (present position); this tells you how far a journey you will need to travel to get where you want to be. Finally, your value includes the strengths you possess (and what you have access to through others) in order to complete your journey.

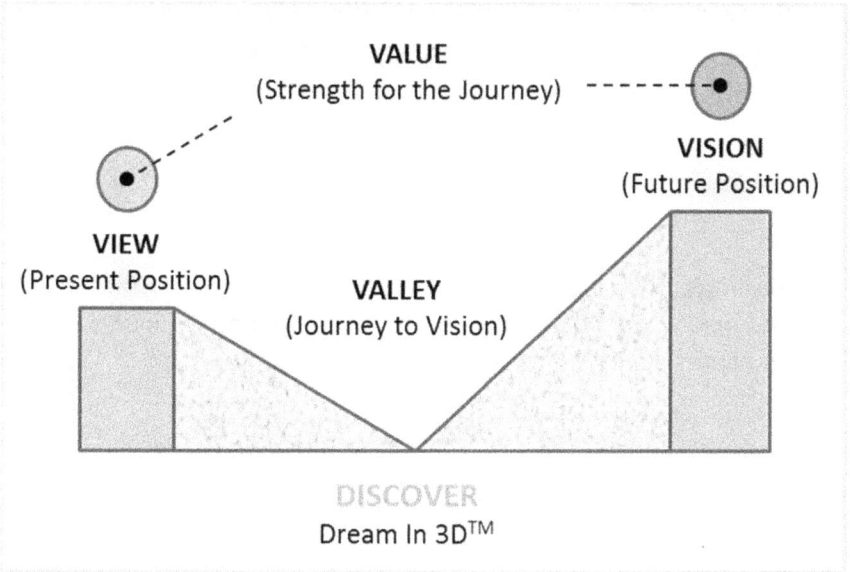

Vision #1: What are my desired facts of life?

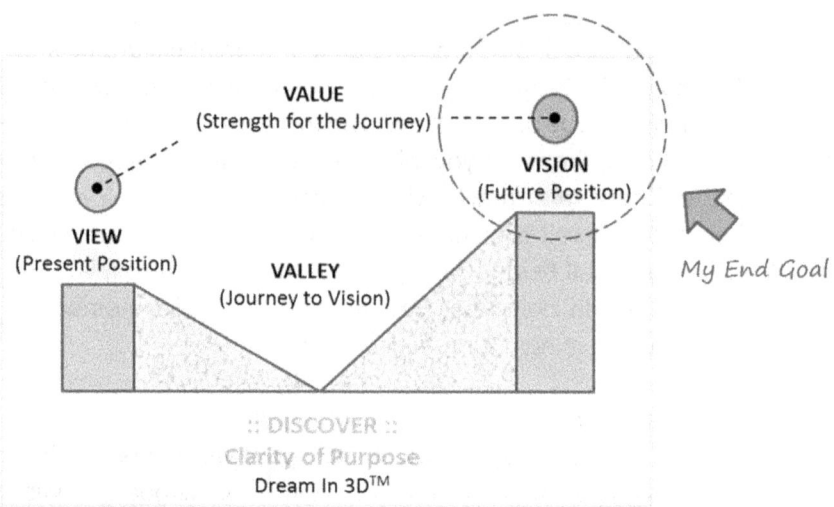

Your vision includes facts that you want to be true about various areas of your life. Typically, we have a belief that these facts will lead to positive feelings we want to experience and/or a level fulfillment and satisfaction with life. Consider the following when reflecting upon your vision:

- **Facts (Milestones)** – What do you want to be true about your life? Think in terms of <u>habits</u> (what you want to do routinely), <u>haves</u> (what you want own), and <u>happenings</u> (what you want achieve).

  _____

  _____

  _____

- **Feelings (Moments)** – How will the facts listed above improve how your experience your life? Think in terms of your desired emotional states.

  _____

  _____

  _____

- **Fulfillment (Monuments)** – How will the facts you listed contribute to the satisfaction and lasting peace that comes with fulfilling your purpose? Think in terms of how the facts are aligned with the principles and purposes that guide your life.

_____

_____

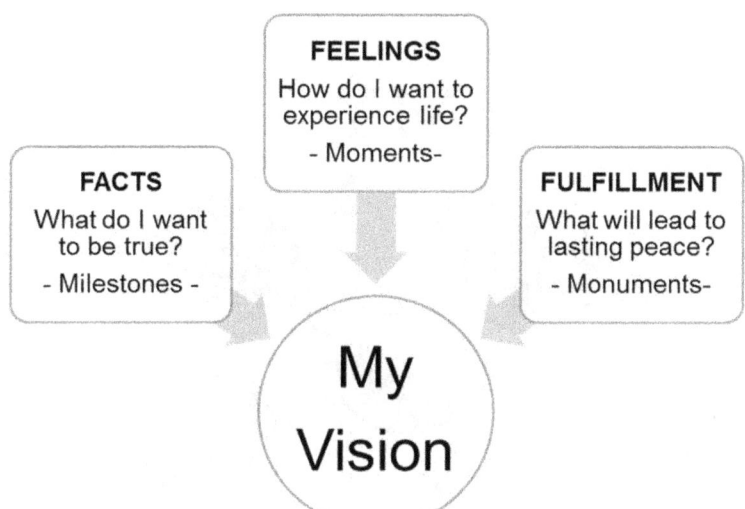

Vision #2: My LIFE'S Legacy
What is your vision for your life? Before you answer that question, be sure that your vision includes each area of your life in order to achieve balanced fulfillment. "**LIFE'S Legacy**" is a starting point for setting goals in each area of your life. It is an acronym that stands for the following:
- **Lifestyle** addresses your physical health, finances, and how you use your free-time (and, believe it or not, all time is free time).
- Your **Interests** include what you desire to learn in life to satisfy your career aspirations, competencies for personal and profession goals, and your general curiosities.
- **Fellowship** looks at your relationships with family, friends, and fellow-citizens with whom you share this world.

- **Experiences** include the personal and professional life events and moments for which you would like to say, "Been there. Done that."
- **Spiritual** focuses upon how you seek out purpose and timeless principles, how you serve others, and how you see and interpret the world around you.
- Finally, **Legacy** is about your contributions that you start upon while living and leave behind once your time on earth has concluded.

Lifestyle ♦ Interests ♦ Fellowship ♦ Experiences ♦ Spirituality

In this section, you will describe what you want to be true in each area of your **LIFE'S Legacy**. It can take some time to truly get a clear vision for your ideal accomplishments in each area of your **LIFE'S Legacy**. Start with the areas that are easiest for you to address; then work your way to the ones that challenge you most.

Using the prompts below, write your vision for each **LIFE'S Legacy** category listed.

Lifestyle – your day-to-day lifestyle

1. Describe your ideal physical condition.

2. Describe your ideal financial position.

3. Describe your ideal use of your free-time.

Interests – your lifelong learning goals

1. Describe your ideal career.

2. Describe your top curiosities (i.e. topics you wish to know more about).

3. Describe your ideal competencies (i.e. desired knowledge and skills).

Fellowship – your relationships

1. Describe your ideal relationship with family.

2. Describe your ideal relationship with friends.

3. Describe your ideal relationship with fellow-citizens (e.g. new acquaintances, peers, extended networks, etc.).

Experiences – your participation in life events

1. What do you wish to experience in your personal life?

2. What do you wish to experience in your professional life?

Spiritual - your pursuit and expression of timeless principles and purposes

1. Describe your ideal spiritual habits.

2. Describe your ideal participation in serving others.

3. Describe how you see the world (e.g. world view, perspectives on life, principles to live by, etc.)

Legacy - your contributions to the world

1. Describe your ideal contribution to yourself (or as a representation of yourself).

2. Describe your ideal contribution to family and friends.

3. Describe your ideal contribution to the world.

Tips for getting the most out of your **LIFE'S Legacy** reflection:
- **Go With Your Gut** – Your vision is yours. Be honest about what you really see for yourself.
- **Be S.M.A.R.T.** – Use specific, measureable, attainable, relevant, and time-bound goals.
- **Find Your Motivation** – Detail what drives you to want a given goal.
- **Visualize Yourself Naturally Enjoying Success** – Imagine what life will look like once you achieve a given goal. As you use your imagination, see what feelings of fulfillment surface for you. Include these in your vision descriptions.
- **Find A Model** – Look for models of others who have achieved a goal that you desire.

- **Start With Easy Wins** – Decide to take action on one of your goals immediately in order to get into the habit of addressing that area of life in your desired manner.
- **Use Pictures and Visual Aides** - Find pictures that represent your vision. For health, maybe you desire to be as fit as a triathelete; so you find a picture of one from Sports Illustrated. For experiences, perhaps you want to travel the world; so you may Google Singapore to find an image to save or find a travel agent who can provide a brochure.

View: What are my present facts of life?

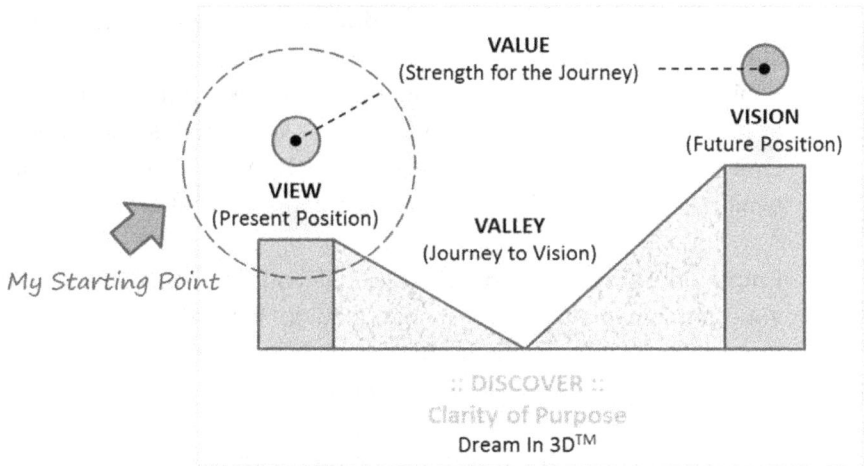

While your Vision focuses on the life you want (in the future), your View refers to the facts of your life as they are right now. Your current facts of life serve as the starting-line for your journey to your dream. When you decide to face your present view, you decide to enter the race.

Knowing where you REALLY are, as compared to where you prefer to THINK you are, is the best motivation to move you in the right direction. Knowing your present view of your facts of life will help you to know where you stand so you know what you need to do to move towards your vision – i.e. your ideal facts of life.

Here are a few considerations when detailing your present view:

- **Focus on facts...JUST THE FACTS.** It is what it is...until it isn't. Do not add negative meanings or prophecies of doom. For example, if you are not physically fit, it will not help for you to meditate on your laiziness, indiscipline, or procrastination. While some of these charactization may be justified by your history, they seldom motivate you to be your best. More so, they reinforce messages about why you may never reach your goal. Just list out the facts so you can focus on what you will do to change those facts. "I am out of shape. It will take a lot of work to get in shape. I will do what it tait, a step at a time."

- **Facts induce fear. Facts also reduce fear.** Knowing where you stand puts a face on the challenges you must overcome to achieve your dream. The challlenges may make you nervous; but at least now you know how to prepare – which helps calm fears. One helpful activity is to research others who have overcome similar challenges. Testimonials help you see what is possible.

- **Facts can inspire follow-through.** If you are dissatisfied with your present view, it can inspire you to follow-through with a greater level of intensity in order to change your circumstances. The more you face your reality and how it makes you feel, the more you will want to make a change.

- **Knowing where you REALLY are keeps you honest, humble, and focused on the matter at hand.** There used to be a saying when I was a child: when you point at someone, there are three fingers pointing back at you. Staying aware of your current view, relative to your own life, tends to help remind you to: (a) take your own advice; (b) preach only what you actually practice; and (c) deal with your own relative shortcomings rather than focusing on the shortcomings of others.

- **You can never really avoid reality.** There may be times when you want avoid reality at all costs. Avoiding reality gives a false sense of peace. Deep down, when avoiding reality, we are normally clear that reality will catch up to us one day. This leads to paranoia. It is not worth it. Just face it so you can move forward.

- **Accepting unpleasant, yet changeable, reality as permanent leads to hopelessness.** As you face an unpleasant reaility, maintain hope that change is possible. The present is a gift – maximize the moment. The fact that you have a present to view means that you are alive and have an opportunity to use your next moment to move in your desired direction. A change in your life facts will rarely if ever be instant; a change in your mindset can be immediate.

- **You may be closer to your dream than you think.** In dealing with your present view, you may find that you are closer to your goal than you originally thought. Success is not a neat process; it is often messy and filled with a few ups and many downs. Progress is not always obvious. However, as you get into the habit of facing the reality of your present facts of life on a consistent basis, you will discover that you often have made progress and that you are closer to the finish line than you thought.

View: What is the current status of my LIFE'S Legacy?
Return to your LIFE'S Legacy exercise that you completed in the section on Vision. As a reminder, your LIFE'S Legacy areas are as follows:

- **Lifestyle** – your day-to-day lifestyle (finances, physical health, and free-time)
- **Interests** – your lifelong learning approach (career, curiosities, competencies)
- **Fellowship** – your relationships (family, friends, fellow-citizens)
- **Experiences** – your participation in life events (personal pleasure, professional)
- **Legacy** – your contributions to the world (gifts for self, family, friends, world)

For each area of your LIFE'S Legacy for which you detailed the facts that you desire for your life, describe your present view of that area of your life.

In other words, list the current status of your goals. Examples are provided for you.

Lifestyle – your day-to-day lifestyle

1. Describe your ideal physical condition.

    _____
    _____
    _____
    _____

2. Describe your ideal financial position.

    _____
    _____
    _____
    _____

3. Describe your ideal use of your free-time.

    _____
    _____
    _____
    _____

Interests – your lifelong learning goals

1. Describe your ideal career.

    _____
    _____
    _____
    _____

2. Describe your top curiosities (i.e. topics you wish to know more about).

    _____
    _____

3. Describe your ideal competencies (i.e. desired knowledge and skills).

Fellowship – your relationships

1. Describe your ideal relationship with family.

2. Describe your ideal relationship with friends.

3. Describe your ideal relationship with fellow-citizens (e.g. new acquaintances, peers, extended networks, etc.).

Experiences – your participation in life events

1. What do you wish to experience in your personal life?

2. What do you wish to experience in your professional life?

Spiritual - your pursuit and expression of timeless principles and purposes

1. Describe your ideal spiritual habits.

2. Describe your ideal participation in serving others.

3. Describe how you see the world (e.g. world view, perspectives on life, principles to live by, etc.)

Legacy - your contributions to the world

1. Describe your ideal contribution to yourself (or as a representation of yourself).

2. Describe your ideal contribution to family and friends.

3. Describe your ideal contribution to the world.

Valley: What will it take to get from my present facts of life to my desired facts of life *(i.e. from my vew to my vision)*?

Your Valley is the distance that exists between where you are at present and where you wish to be; it is the gap that exists between your vision and your present view. Your Valley represents the journey you will take as you pursue your dream lifestyle; it gives you an idea of what it will take to achieve your dream.

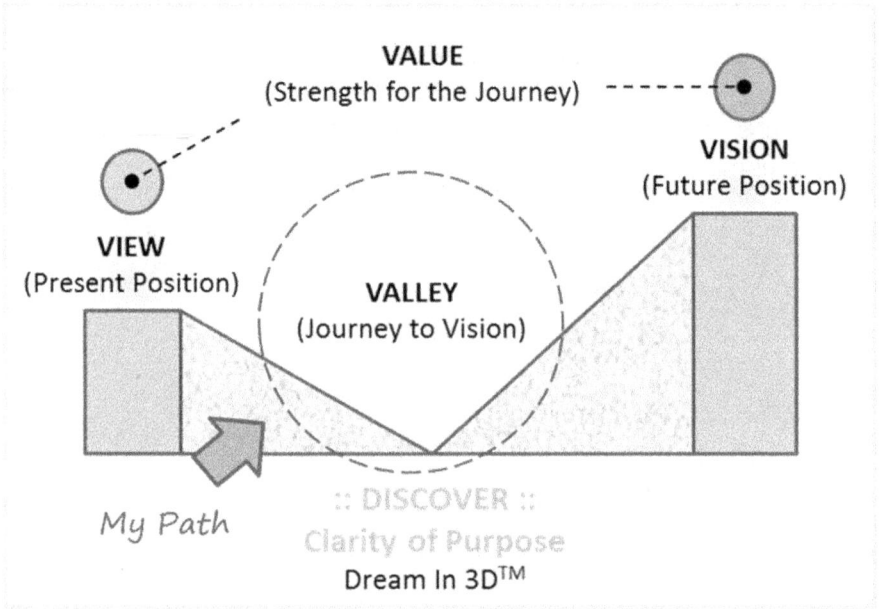

The quality of your dream-fulfillment plan greatly depends upon your accurate awareness of your Valley. Knowing the work you must complete in order to achieve your dream allows you to:

- Set realistic expectations and timelines
- Prepare for challenges
- Determine the best course of action to take
- Divide your dream into smaller goals that you will achieve along the way to your ultimate destination; this will allow you to recognize and celebrate your progress, build momentum, and increase confidence that your dream will become a reality.

Valley Exercise: How close am I to the finish line?
Return to the LIFE'S Legacy exercises that you completed in the sections on Vision and View.

As a reminder, your LIFE'S Legacy areas are as follows:

- **Lifestyle** – your day-to-day lifestyle (finances, physical health, and free-time)
- **Interests** – your lifelong learning approach (career, curiosities, competencies)
- **Fellowship** – your relationships (family, friends, fellow-citizens)
- **Experiences** – your participation in life events (personal pleasure, professional)
- **Legacy** – your contributions to the world (gifts for self, family, friends, world)

For each area of your LIFE'S Legacy for which you detailed your Vision (i.e. desired facts of life) and View (i.e. present facts of life), finish the process by detailing how far you have to go in order to reach your ultimate dream. Then, when possible, divide that dream into doable goals that will allow you to celebrate progress over time. Examples are provided for you.

Lifestyle – your day-to-day lifestyle

1. Describe your ideal physical condition.

2. Describe your ideal financial position.

3. Describe your ideal use of your free-time.

Interests – your lifelong learning goals

1. Describe your ideal career.

   _____
   _____
   _____
   _____

2. Describe your top curiosities (i.e. topics you wish to know more about).

   _____
   _____
   _____
   _____

3. Describe your ideal competencies (i.e. desired knowledge and skills).

   _____
   _____
   _____
   _____

Fellowship – your relationships

1. Describe your ideal relationship with family.

   _____
   _____
   _____
   _____

2. Describe your ideal relationship with friends.

   _____
   _____
   _____

_____
_____

3. Describe your ideal relationship with fellow-citizens (e.g. new acquaintances, peers, extended networks, etc.).

_____
_____
_____
_____

Experiences – your participation in life events

1. What do you wish to experience in your personal life?

_____
_____
_____
_____

2. What do you wish to experience in your professional life?

_____
_____
_____
_____

Spiritual - your pursuit and expression of timeless principles and purposes

1. Describe your ideal spiritual habits.

_____
_____
_____
_____

2. Describe your ideal participation in serving others.

3. Describe how you see the world (e.g. world view, perspectives on life, principles to live by, etc.)

Legacy - your contributions to the world

1. Describe your ideal contribution to yourself (or as a representation of yourself).

2. Describe your ideal contribution to family and friends.

3. Describe your ideal contribution to the world.

Value: What resources can I leverage in order to achieve my dream?

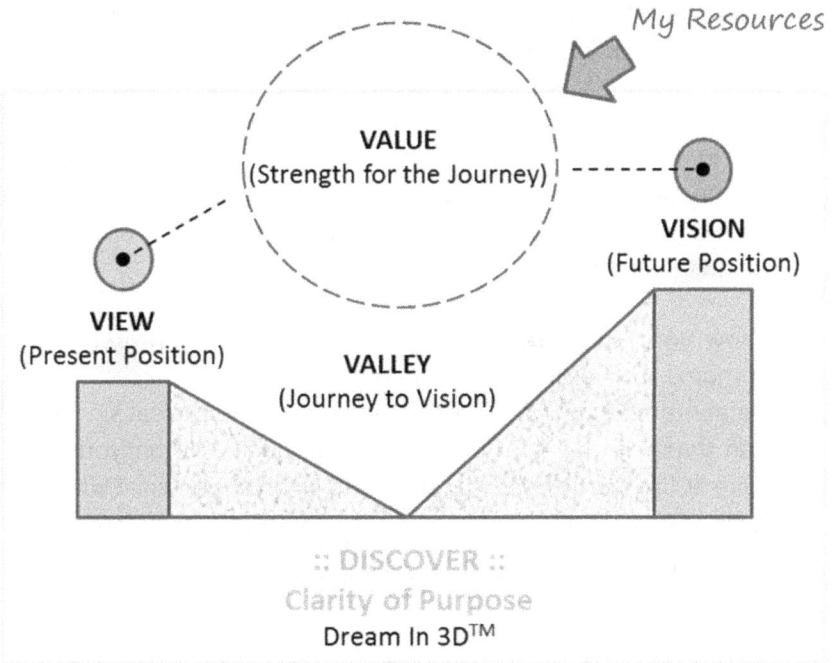

Your Value is a combination of the *resources you possess* and the *resources that you put to good use*. It is important that you know and appreciate what is *available* for your use and that you *apply* it towards achieving your desired facts of life. Knowing your value gives you strength for your journey to your vision.

- **Know that you have value**. You have value just by virtue of your being. There are, however, characteristics of your value that are more helpful than others based upon specific situations. It is important to be clear on the value you possess and how to use that for achieving your dreams.

- **Know your story.** Your personal story gives clues about the characteristics of your values. In reflecting upon your story, you bring to surface the strengths and skills you have applied in life, to-date.

- **Know your strengths.** You have talents that seem to come natural to you, that you most enjoy doing, and that you have used over time in many situations. These are your strengths. Know your strengths and how you can use them to reach your dream.

- **Know your skills.** There are specific abilitites that you learned how to do. These are your skills. Common skills include working with people, working with objectives, and working with information / ideas. It is important to know and apply all of your skills when pursuing your dreams.

- **Know your sources of support.** You may have a great story, strengths, and skills, but you cannot do it all by yourself. There are some strengths and skills that you do not possess. Rather than trying to develop those strengths and skills on your own, invite willing participants to cooperate with you to assist with your goals. Know who is around you, what they have to offer, and how they may be willing to support your dream.

- **Know your surroundings.** Know your assets – the resources around you that can contribute to the fulfillment of your dream. Often times, there are businesses, community organizations, places of worship, government departments, online communities, and other such resources that are available to help you with some aspect of what you are trying to do.

- **Make the most of your value**. Follow-through is the key. You do not need to be superhuman; nor do you need to possess all of the skills and talents of another person. Simply use what you posses (or have access to) and do so with consistency.

- **You can always create more value.** You have the capacity to grow and develop. Appreciate and maximize the value that you already have; use that as a foundation. Then, set goals to improve yourself over time.

KNOW YOUR VALUE

Value Exercise: How will I use what I have to get where I want to be?
The following is a set of exercises that will help you discover and describe characteristics of your Value. There are a few things to keep in mind while completing the exercises:
- Be honest
- Be realistic
- Be confident
- Be yourself

Enjoy the process of knowing your Value!

▶ Value Exercise 1: Know Your Story

Often times, the characteristics of your value surface when you tell your story. Take a moment to reflect upon your life story – particularly times when you have applied various strengths to accomplish a desired end – no matter what that end was AND regardless of whether or not you were officially recognized for your efforts. There are some prompts below that will help you.

Story 1. Think about a time you were called upon to provide someone with help for a given situation. What were you asked to do? How did the person know you were the right person to call?

How did you approach the task (be specific)? What was the outcome of the situation? What does this story tell you about your value to others?

Story 2. Think about a time when you had a goal you wanted to accomplish. What were you hoping to accomplish? How did you figure that you had what it took in order to achieve the goal? How did you approach the task (be specific)? What was the outcome of the situation? What does this story tell you about your ability to achieve a goal?

Story 3. Think about a time when you felt defeated by life circumstances. Perhaps you lost in a competition or was looked over for a promotion. Maybe you did not get a grade in school that you desired or you had some trouble with a relationship. What was the situation? Describe how you were able to move forward despite the situation? What does this story tell you about your ability to overcome adversity?

▶ **Value Exercise 2: Know Your Strengths**

Below is a list of strength categories and descriptions. For each item, put a check mark for the ones that apply to you and a double check mark for the ones which are truly great fit. List your top five strengths. This stregnths list was sourced from: http://www.meaningandhappiness.com/psychology-research/list-of-personal-strengths.html

A. **Strengths of Wisdom and Knowledge** - Cognitive strengths that entail the acquisition and use of knowledge

- ☐ **Creativity [originality, ingenuity]**: Thinking of novel and productive ways to conceptualize and do things.

- ☐ **Curiosity [interest, novelty-seeking, openness to experience]**: Taking an interest in ongoing experience for its own sake; exploring and discovering.

- ☐ **Open-mindedness [judgment, critical thinking]**: Thinking things through and examining them from all sides; weighing all evidence fairly.

- ☐ **Love of learning**: Mastering new skills, topics, and bodies of knowledge, whether on one's own or formally.

- ☐ **Perspective [wisdom]**: Being able to provide wise counsel to others; having ways of looking at the world that make sense to oneself and to other people.

B. **Strengths of Courage** - Emotional strengths that involve the exercise of will to accomplish goals in the face of opposition, external and internal.

- ☐ **Bravery [valor]**: Not shrinking from threat, challenge, difficulty, or pain; acting on convictions even if unpopular.

- ☐ **Persistence [perseverance, industriousness]**: Finishing what one starts; persisting in a course of action in spite of obstacles.

- [ ] **Integrity [authenticity, honesty]**: Presenting oneself in a genuine way; taking responsibility for one's feeling and actions.

- [ ] **Vitality [zest, enthusiasm, vigor, energy]**: Approaching life with excitement and energy; feeling alive and activated.

C. **Strengths of Humanity** - interpersonal strengths that involve tending and befriending others

- [ ] **Love**: Valuing close relations with others, in particular those in which sharing and caring are reciprocated.

- [ ] **Kindness [generosity, nurturance, care, compassion, altruistic love, "niceness"]**: Doing favors and good deeds for others.

- [ ] **Social intelligence [emotional intelligence, personal intelligence]**: Being aware of the motives and feelings of other people and oneself.

D. **Strengths of Justice** - civic strengths that underlie healthy community life

- [ ] **Citizenship [social responsibility, loyalty, teamwork]**: Working well as a member of a group or team; being loyal to the group.

- [ ] **Fairness**: Treating all people the same according to notions of fairness and justice; not letting personal feelings bias decisions about others.

- [ ] **Leadership**: Encouraging a group of which one is a member to get things done and at the same maintain time good relations within the group.

E. **Strengths of Temperance** - strengths that protect against excess

- ☐ **Forgiveness and mercy**: Forgiving those who have done wrong; accepting the shortcomings of others; giving people a second chance; not being vengeful.

- ☐ **Humility / Modesty**: Letting one's accomplishments speak for themselves; not regarding oneself as more special than one is.

- ☐ **Prudence**: Being careful about one's choices; not taking undue risks; not saying or doing things that might later be regretted.

- ☐ **Self-regulation [self-control]**: Regulating what one feels and does; being disciplined; controlling one's appetites and emotions.

F. **Strengths of Transcendence** - strengths that forge connections to the larger universe and provide meaning

- ☐ **Appreciation of beauty and excellence [awe, wonder, elevation]**: Appreciating beauty, excellence, and/or skilled performance in various domains of life.

- ☐ **Gratitude**: Being aware of and thankful of the good things that happen; taking time to express thanks.

- ☐ **Hope [optimism, future-mindedness, future orientation]**: Expecting the best in the future and working to achieve it.

- ☐ **Humor [playfulness]**: Liking to laugh and tease; bringing smiles to other people; seeing the light side.

- ☐ **Spirituality [religiousness, faith, purpose]**: Having coherent beliefs about the higher purpose, the meaning of life, and the meaning of the universe.

Based upon the strengths that you checked, list the your top five strengths below:

▶ **Value Exercise 3: Know Your Skills**

Below is a list of skills sourced from the Career Services Department at the University of Toledo (http://www.utoledo.edu/utlc/career/pdfs/transferable_skills_checklist.pdf). Put a check by the skills you you possess; double check your strongest skills.

- ☐ **Interpersonal skills** - able to interact successfully with a wide range of people; knows how to interpret and use body language

- ☐ **Oral communication skills** - presents information and ideas clearly and concisely, with content and style appropriate for the audience (whether one-to-one or in a group); presents opinions and ideas in an open, objective way

- ☐ **Public speaking skills** - able to make formal presentations; presents ideas, positions and problems in an interesting way

- ☐ **Counseling skills** - responds to what others have said in a non-judgmental way ("active listening"); builds trust and openness with others

- ☐ **Coaching / mentoring skills** - gives feedback in a constructive way; helps others to increase their knowledge or skills

- ☐ **Teaching / training skills** - able to help others gain knowledge and skills; able to create an effective learning environment

- ☐ **Supervising skills** - delegates responsibilities and establishes an appropriate system of accountability; able to monitor progress and assess the quality of job performance of others

- **Leadership skills** - motivates and empowers others to act; inspires trust and respect in others

- **Persuading skills** - communicates effectively to justify a position or influence a decision; able to sell products or promote ideas

- **Negotiating skills** - able to negotiate skillfully; knows how and when to make compromises

- **Mediation skills** - able to resolve conflicts that stems from different perspectives or interests; able to deal with conflict in an open, honest and positive way

- **Interviewing skills** - asks and responds to questions effectively; able to make others feel relaxed and to create a feeling of trust

- **Customer service skills** - able to build a relationship of mutual trust with clients; able to handle complaints and concerns in a sensitive way

- **Care-giving skills** - able to empathize with others; able to give sensitive care to people who are sick or elderly or who have severe disabilities

- **Analytical / logical thinking skills** - able to draw specific conclusions from a set of general observations or from a set of specific facts; able to synthesize information and ideas

- **Critical thinking skills** - able to review different points of view or ideas and make objective judgments; investigates all possible solutions to a problem, weighing the pros and cons

- **Creative thinking skills** - able to generate new ideas, invent new things, create new images or designs; find new solutions to problems; able to use wit and humor effectively

- **Problem-solving skills** - able to clarify the nature of a problem, evaluate alternatives, propose viable solutions and determine the outcome of the various options

- **Decision-making skills** - able to identify all possible options, weigh the pros and cons, assess feasibility and choose the most viable option

- **Planning skills** - able to plan projects, events and programs; able to establish objectives and needs, evaluates options, chooses best option

- **Organizational skills** - able to organize information, people or things in a systematic way; able to establish priorities and meet deadlines

- **Advanced writing skills** - able to select, interpret, organize and synthesize key ideas; able to edit a written text to ensure that the message is as clear, concise and accurate as possible

- **Research skills** - knows how to find and collect relevant background information; able to analyze data, summarize findings and write a report

- **Financial skills** - able to keep accurate financial records; able to manage a budget (that is, preparing sound budgets and monitoring expenses)

- **Language skills** - functionally bilingual; able to translate and/or interpret in a given language

- **Advanced computer skills** - able to use a variety of software programs; knowledge about desk-top publishing or web design

- **Technological skills** - understands technical systems and operates effectively within them; understands technical specifications; reads technical manuals with ease

- **Performing skills** - able to make presentations for video or television in an interesting way; able to entertain, amuse and inspire an audience

- **Artistic skills** - uses color and design creatively; able to design displays and publicity material (print, video, Internet)

- **Perceptual skills** - able to visualize new formats and shapes; able to estimate physical space

☐ **Mechanical skills** - able to install, operate and monitor the performance of equipment and mechanical devices; able to repair mechanical devices

☐ **Adaptability skills** - capacity to adapt to new situations and settings and to tolerate change well; flexibility to adapt to the needs of the moment

☐ **Administrative / clerical skills** - able to operate computers and other basic office equipment; able to design and maintain filing and control systems

Now that you have identified your skills, list your top five skills below.

_____
_____
_____
_____
_____

▶ **Value Exercise 4: Know Your Sources of Support**

List 10 people who can be of support to you in one way or another as your pursue your dreams. This list can include family, friends, mentors, coaches, teachers, counselors, peers, co-workers, employers, employees, etc. Write the name and what value each person may contribute towards your goal.

_____
_____
_____
_____

▶ **Value Exercise 5: Know Your Surroundings**

List 10 businesses and organizations that can be of support to you in one way or another as your pursue your dreams. This list can include government departments, schools, product or service providers, libraries, social programs, places of worship, etc.. Write the name and what value each business or organization may contribute towards your goal.

_____
_____
_____
_____

Next Steps
1. Review key concepts from this section:

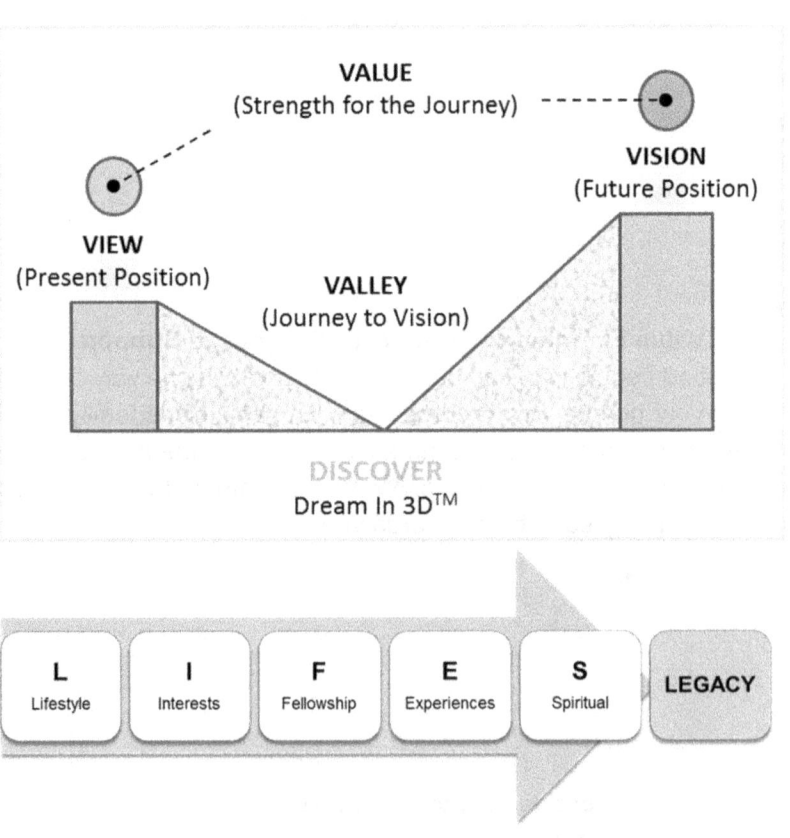

2. Share your completed Discover My Purpose exercises with family, friends, and other peers.

3. Reflect on the following:
   - What did you discover about your LIFE'S Legacy vision as a result of the exercises?

     _____
     _____
     _____

   - What did you learn about your value as a result of the exercises?

     _____
     _____
     _____

   - Which LIFE'S Legacy areas were most challenging for you to complete?

     _____
     _____
     _____

   - Commit to reviewing your LIFE's Legacy items daily for the next 90 days.

   - Re-write vision, view, valley, and value statements for 1 of your top goals from your LIFE'S Legacy exercises:

     _____
     _____
     _____

Process 2
DEVELOP MY PATHS

Once you have made your desired vision known and visible, it is time to make it real and tangible. **Develop My Paths** is the process by which you apply available resources towards bringing your dream from a mental concept to a concrete reality. You identify options, develop a plan to maximize opportunities, and then take action to make your dream come true.

Developing paths to your dreams requires that you:

- **Exercise your creative muscles**. We are designed to create; however, we sometimes default to submitting to circumstances instead. Get used to creating!

- **Be disciplined**. While creativity can be fun, there are also very mundane aspects that are not always fun in the moment. Normally, there are a set of key activities that must be repeated in order to bring about the dream fulfillment that you seek. You must be willing to develop habits necessary and to follow successful, proven models and principles – even on the days that you do not feel like doing so OR would rather be doing something more fun.

- **Get used to taking action in the midst of uncertainty.** It is easier for us to walk into a situation that is already set-up for us – even if it is not the most ideal circumstance, it gives us an emotional break from dealing with some of the unknowns associated with creating our own situation. During the process, you find yourself investing in activities – but not really knowing, with 100% certainty, how things are going to turn out. We have to move forward with faith.

- **Focus**. There is a limitless number of opportunities that compete for your time and attention; however, you are working with a limited amount of time and resources. You have to decide what matters most to you and which opportunities are most worthy of your participation. Once you make those decisions, you need to carry your plans through to completion. There will be many distractions and temptations to divert from your path. You will also have times where you will want to multitask in order to accomplish many goal at once so you can speed up your process. Fight those urges as much as possible. Focus on 1-3 major goals at a time. Allow yourself to time necessary to fully follow- through on plans. Finish what you start.

- **Get comfortable with change**. Opportunities, strategies, and plans look neat on paper. Making things happen is often messier experience. By the time you finish, you may find that you made several adjustments to your planned activities. Get comfortable with change. View the development process as an experiment during which Yukon do your best to plan and predict outcomes, but you do not really know how things will work out until you take action. Be open to making change as needed.

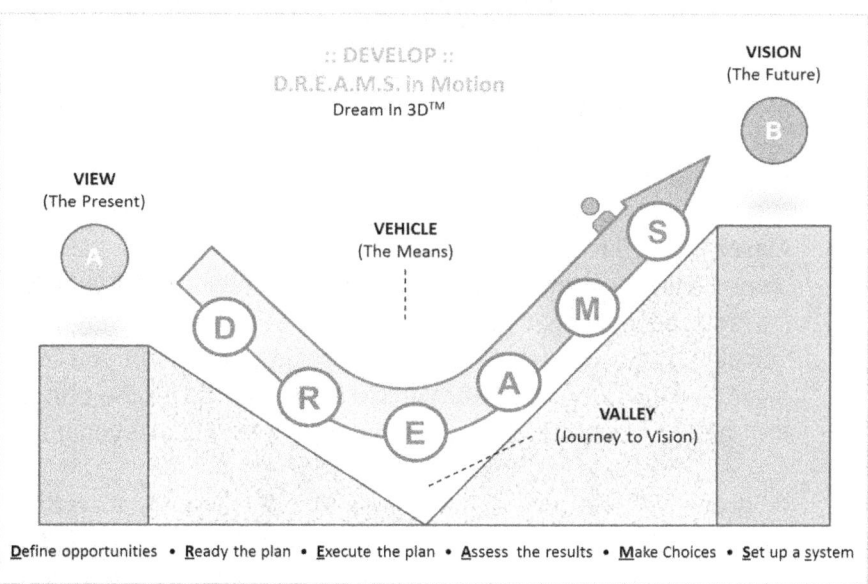

Define opportunities • **R**eady the plan • **E**xecute the plan • **A**ssess the results • **M**ake Choices • **S**et up a **s**ystem

Finding Your Vehicles (Part 1): Yea though I walk, run, drive, fly, sail, cycle, or ski through the valley…

"Developing My Paths" is mainly about finding ways to get from where you are (at present) to where you want to be (in the future). As discussed in the section, "Discover My Purpose," when you begin your pursuit of a dream, you identify your vision (your desired facts of life) and your present view (your current facts of life). The gap between your view and your vision is referred to as your valley – i.e. the distance between your starting point and your end goal. Any activity or resource that you use to get you to your goal is referred to as your vehicle - i.e. your means to an end. Your vision is a clear picture of where you want to go; your vehicle is what gets you there. Decide now to become a pro at finding vehicles that will best transport you to your destination in life.

There are several keys to finding your vehicles:

- **Do not reinvent the vehicle; just customize it**. Find models that are similar to what you wish to accomplish and borrow the parts that work. There is no need to reinvent the wheel. However, you may need to customize it to your liking.

- **It may take several paths and vehicles to get to your goal**. Ideally, it would be most convenient to be able to leverage one vehicle for the entire journey. In many cases, this may be possible. However, what I have discovered is that different parts of the valley may require us to leverage a different vehicle for that part of the journey.

- **Marry the vision. Divorce the vehicle**. I normally tell my students to marry the vision and just make friends with the vehicle. Do not become identified with one vehicle. You are not your vehicle. The purpose of a given vehicle is to transport you to a given destination. Whatever vehicle is best suited for the part of the valley you are currently up to, that is the vehicle that you take.

- **A great vehicle does not guarantee a smooth traveling experience**. You may find a great vehicle that has the potential to get you where you wish to go in life. However, the path you travel upon may have a few obstacles, potholes, and unexpected twists and turns. The journey to your dream will not be smooth, in most cases. Expect challenges.

- **There is no perfect vehicle**. There is no opportunity or plan that is perfect, in and of itself. You will likely need to make adjustments as your travel down the paths that lead to your dreams.

- **A great vehicle still needs a great owner / driver**. Read the manual. Know your vehicle well. Operate your vehicle according to best practice.

Driving Your Vehicles (Part 2): Setting your D.R.E.A.M.S. in motion
The D.R.E.A.M.S. model is a step-by-step process for designing and driving the vehicles that will carry you from your "view" to your "vision." D.R.E.A.M.S. provides a set of general tasks to be completed in pursuit of any opportunity that promises to help us reach a stated goal:

- **Define opportunities** - identify and evaluate options for pursuing, and achieving, a given goal;

- **Ready your plan** - outline a step-by-step plan for maximizing a selected opportunity;

- **Execute your plan** - complete the steps that you outlined;

- **Assess your results** - evaluate what you accomplished;

- **Make choices** - based upon results, decide to stick with what you are doing or take a different approach; and

- **Set up a system** - identify your best opportunities and steps; make them part of your regular routine.

Below please find additional details for each step in the D.R.E.A.M.S. process.

▶ **Define Opportunities**
You must define the opportunity. An opportunity is any action, or set of activities, that you believe will help you achieve a given goal A complete opportunity should be able to progress you from your "view" through the valley" all the way to your vision.

When you decide to pursue a dream (i.e. a vision, goal), you have to make choices about how best to invest your time, energy, emotions, and resources. The idea is to select the opportunity that fits you best and for which you are most positioned to profit.

To define an opportunity, ask questions like:

- What is the opportunity?
- How will the opportunity help me reach my goal (i.e. dream, vision)?
- What resources do I need to make the opportunity work as it should?
- How long will it take for me to see results from this opportunity?
- How well am I positioned to take advantage of this opportunity?
- How much influence do I have over the success of this opportunity?
- What are the top alternatives to this opportunity? How do they compare?
- How will working on this opportunity affect other areas of my life?
- Once you have an opportunity worth your time, it is time to Ready Your Plan.

▶ **Ready Your Plan**

Now that you have defined the opportunity and decided to move forward with it, you will need a personalized, step-by-step action plan for making the opportunity work for you. It is important that you consider all the steps necessary and how you will complete the steps.

If there are steps that you do not want to complete, or that you cannot complete for some reason, you will need to determine how that will impact your intended results and whether the opportunity is still worth your time. In many cases, you will have to complete the opportunity exactly as prescribed. However, in some cases, you may be able to substitute steps with solid alternatives and still achieve intended results.

Your plan will include:

- A clear statement of your goal – the fact(s) that you want to be true once you complete the opportunity
- The steps required for the opportunity –actions and activities that need to be done
- The timeline – due dates for each step and the order in which you are to complete the steps
- The resources – the people, information, skills, money, time, and tools needed to successfully complete each step
- The back-up plan – a realistic list of potential challenges you may face and alternatives for meeting your goals

Now that you have an action plan, "Execute" it!

▶ Execute Your Plan

A plan only has value when you actually execute it. Your ability to execute a plan separates day dreamers from those who Dream In 3-D. Follow-through separates those who simply conceive ideas from those who actually complete ideas. Fidelity (i.e. faithfulness in execution of your plan) is key for realizing maximum results from your opportunity and achieving your end goal.

You execute best when you:

- Post the details of the opportunity and objectives in a place where you will see it often throughout the day
- Schedule each step – making sure that you have allowed enough time for completion
- Keep a journal where you can chart your progress including steps you completes along with any challenges and how you will overcome them
- Celebrate completed steps – each moment leads to momentum, so enjoy each completed step

- Stick to the facts – whether you successfully completed steps or skipped steps, simply detail what you did and what you need to do next
- Have a short memory. When you succeed, enjoy the moment, but then move on so as not to get complacent. When you fail, accept reality, but then move on – so as not to get depressed (i.e. stuck)

After you execute your plan, it is time to "Assess" the results.

▶ Assess your results

The whole point of an opportunity is that, once completed, it progresses you towards your desired vision. Therefore, once you set up a roadmap and execute your plan, it is time to Assess how far you have come since the time you started on the opportunity.

- Where did you start?
- Where were you trying to go?
- How far did you make it?
- Did you arrive where you expected to be?
- How much farther do you have to go in order to reach your destination?

These are the key questions to ask when you Assess your progress.

It is very important to assess your progress as accurately as possible. Your vision depends on it. You need to know if the opportunity works for you or if you need to try something new (either because the opportunity is lacking or because you are not committed to it and may need an alternative approach that you are more likely to execute). Here are a few keys to assessing results:

- Restate the objective – what was the promise and goal of the opportunity
- Review your action plan and execution – what was the action plan and how much of it did I complete
- Results – what facts did I achieve

Based upon your results, you will "Make Choices" about the opportunity going forward.

▶ Make Choices: Repeat or Delete Steps

The final two steps of the D.R.E.A.M.S. deal with lifestyle – taking your most successful activities and making them a regular part of your way of life. Before doing so, you will want to make certain that your chosen opportunities, plans, and activities produced the result(s) that you desired. Based upon that assessment, you will Make Choices as to whether you repeat the steps or delete the steps.

If you achieved the desired results from the opportunity, you will do one of two things:

- Repeat the steps according to the original action plan (meaning that the opportunity worked fine for you, as-is); or

- Repeat the steps with some adjustments to the original roadmap (meaning the opportunity works overall, but some changes in approach are needed in order to produce better results).

This is where charting your activities makes a difference as you pinpoint which steps to keep, tweak, or delete.

If you have not achieved the desired results from the opportunity, you will tweak or delete the steps or possibly pursue an alternative option.

As mentioned in the last section, there are times when the issue was not the opportunity itself, but rather it was your poor follow-through. In this case, you still would want to delete or tweak the steps if you are not realistically going to execute them. It is better to come up with a more realistic plan that you will do, then to continue with a great plan that will you are not committed to executing.

Once you decide to to repeat specific activities, set up a System.

▶ Set Up A System: Make your best steps part of your lifestyle

You defined an opportunity. You drafted an action plan and executed it. You assessed the results and made a choice to repeat the steps in order to repeat these results. It is now time for the System.

A System is a set of related practices working together for a given purpose. Since you have already worked through the opportunity, you pretty much have an idea of the practices that work for you. To make it a system simply means that you will purposely make the opportunity (i.e. the action and activities, the steps) a regular part of your lifestyle.

For example, at some point you were taught how to tie a shoe. By the time you became an adult, you do not have to think through each step for tying a shoe; you just do it – seemingly without giving it much thought at all. In the same way, once you have successful steps for meeting a particular goal, you'll want to get it to the point where you do those steps without having to give it much thought at all. You become so accustomed to the steps that you barely have to think about them. The same goes for working towards your dreams. There are activities that work best for helping you achieve your goals.

- Identify the steps that worked best.
- Practice these steps to improve your performance and results.
- Repeat these steps and make them part of your lifestyle.

As you continue to practice the D.R.E.A.M.S. approach, all of these steps, themselves, will become natural and function on autopilot.

Develop My Paths / D.R.E.A.M.S. Profiler

This is brief survey designed to gain initial insights about your approach to setting up a D.R.E.A.M.S. for your various goals – i.e. steps for getting you from where you are to where you want to be. Using your best judgment, rate yourself for each of the following statements. The rating scale is as follows:

- ☑ Place a check mark in the box for each statement that you do well.
- ☒ Place an "x" in the box for each statement that you do sometimes but know you need to do a little extra.
- ☐ Leave a box blank if you never do that item but need to start.

Category 1: Define opportunities
- ☐ I clearly define how an opportunity will benefit me (before I invest my resources).
- ☐ I define my best alternatives before I invest time and energy in an opportunity.
- ☐ I define how much influence I have over the outcome of an opportunity.

Category 2: Ready your plan
- ☐ I draft an action plan (specific steps and timeline) for any opportunity I pursue.
- ☐ I detail the resources needed (and how I will acquire them) for my action plan.
- ☐ I prepare my back-up plan in case things do not go as I originally imagined.

Category 3: Execute the plan
- ☐ Once I draft a action plan, I follow-through on every detail, 100%.
- ☐ When I execute a plan, I keep track of what I completed.
- ☐ I schedule my activities to ensure I prioritize steps that are critical to fulfilling my dream.

Category 4: Assess your results
- ☐ I track my results and compared them to my original goal.
- ☐ I track my completed activities and compare them to my original plan.
- ☐ I focus on the so I always have an accurate picture of my progress.

Category 5: Make Choices
- ☐ When I complete a successful project, I repeat the steps.
- ☐ When I complete a successful projects, but feel it could be better, I adjust the steps.
- ☐ When a project is unsuccessful, I delete the previous set-of-steps & try a new approach.

Category 6: Set up a system
- ☐ I convert my most successful steps into a new lifestyle approach.
- ☐ I develop my own set of successful principles that govern my lifestyle.
- ☐ I publish a set of practices and procedures that remind me of my successful steps.

# of checks (☑) _____   # of x's (☒) _____   # of blanks (☐) _____

The more ☑'s you have, the more closely you are aligned with a balanced D.R.E.A.M.S. profile. If you do not have as many ☑'s as you would like, decide now to do what it takes to make all of the statements a part of your routine.

Next Steps
1. Review key concepts from this section:

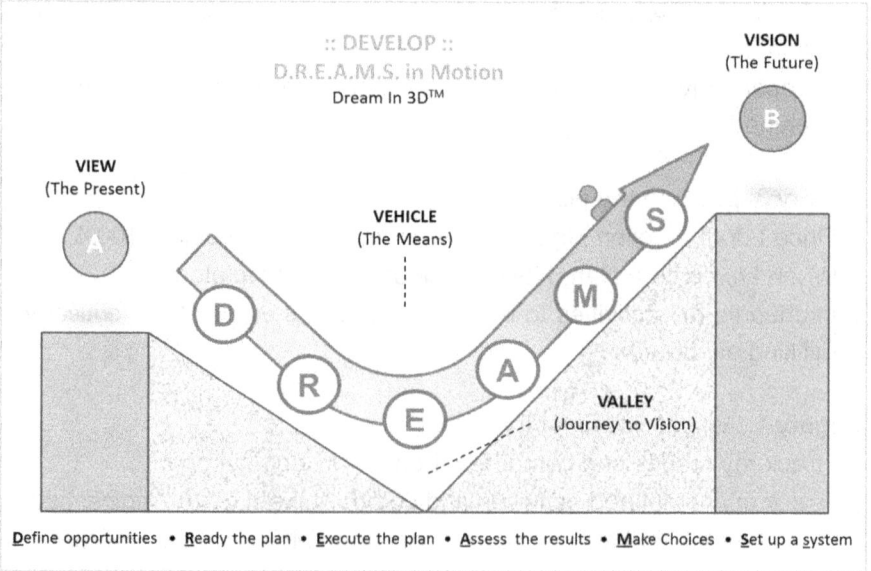

2. Return to one of your top LIFE'S Legacy goal areas (as you already listed on page 42). Write out a D.R.E.A.M.S. plan for that goal and track it for the next 30 days.

   This is my D.R.E.A.M.S. plan for the following goal:

   _____
   _____

   ▶ **Define Opportunities**

   - What is one opportunity (i.e. strategy, set of activities) that I can help me reach my goal? How will this opportunity help me?

     _____
     _____
     _____

   - What resources do I need to make the opportunity work as it should?

     _____
     _____
     _____

   - How long will it take for me to see results from this opportunity?

     _____
     _____
     _____

   - How well am I positioned / prepared to maximize this opportunity?

     _____
     _____
     _____

- How much control do I have over the success of this opportunity?

  _____
  _____

- How will working on this opportunity affect other areas of my life?

  _____
  _____

- What are two alternatives to this opportunity?

  _____
  _____

▶ **Ready Your Plan**

- What fact do you want to be true once you complete the opportunity?

  _____
  _____

- The steps / tasks need to be done *(within the next 30 days)*?

  _____
  _____

- What are the deadlines each step listed above and the order in which you are to complete the steps?

  _____
  _____

- What resources (people, information, skills, money, time, tools) do you need to complete each step?

- The back-up plan — a realistic list of potential challenges you may face and alternatives for meeting your goals

▶ **Execute Your Plan**

- Where will you post the details of your plan so that you are reminded of your goal, objectives, and steps on a daily basis?

- What scheduling tool(s) will you use to schedule your steps and deadlines? Schedule all of your activities now.

- What tool(s) will you use record the steps you completed along with any reflections about, challenges, successes and shortcomings.

- How will I celebrate my successfully completed steps?

  _____
  _____

- Remember: When you succeed, enjoy the moment, but then move on so as not to get complacent. When you fail, accept reality, but then move on – so as not to get depressed (i.e. stuck)

▶ Assess your results

To be completed after 30 days (or whenever you reasonably expected to see results based on your action plan).

- Where did you start? Where were you trying to go? How far did you make it? Did you arrive where you expected to be?

  _____
  _____

- How much farther do you have to go in order to reach your destination?

  _____
  _____

▶ Make Choices: Repeat, Tweak, or Delete Steps

- Which activities or steps would you repeat exactly as originally planned?

  _____
  _____

- Which activities or steps would you tweak (or adjust) going forward?

  _____
  _____
  _____

- Which activities or steps would you delete, altogether?

  _____
  _____
  _____

▶ **Set Up A System: Make your best steps part of your lifestyle**

- Which activities or steps worked best.

  _____
  _____
  _____

- How can you improve your performance and results.

  _____
  _____
  _____

- How will you work these activities and steps into your daily (weekly, month, etc) routine?

  _____
  _____
  _____

Process 3
DISTRIBUTE THROUGH PEOPLE

In most cases, you will experience the most progress when you involve others in bringing D.R.E.A.M.S. to life. **Distribute Through People** is the process by which you share your D.R.E.A.M.S. with people in a manner that inspires them to share their resources to help you achieve your vision. These people are referred to as your "Champions" in that they help you succeed.

There are two primary ways that people will participate with your dream.

- **People SHARE-IN your dream (benefit from the dream)**
  To share in the dream means that the a given person is the recipient of the dream's benefits.

  For example, lets say the dream is your fitness. Someone may witness your physical improvements as they see you walk down the street and it may be pleasing to the sight. Yet, another person (e.g. like a family member, co-worker, etc.) may benefit from your increased energy, enthusiasm, and confidence as applied to joint activities.

  People who share in your dream want to see it come to pass because as the dream benefits you, it benefits them also.

- **People HAVE SHARES IN your dream (build up the dream)**
  To have shares in the dream speaks to a given person taking ownership in the dream – meaning, this person participates in helping to further develop the dream to its full maturity.

  Normally, a person will help build up your dream based upon one or more of the following reasons:

  a) *The person already benefits from what your dream offers and now wants to help to make it better.* By making it better, the person will experience more benefits (for example, a customer giving you feedback to improve your product, or family members helping you with errands so that you will have more free-time to spend with them);

b) *The person shares a passion for the dream or certain aspects it.* By helping you, the person experiences the fulfillment of participating of activity of interest (for example, you want to build a web site with helpful financial information and a real estate professional submits a first-time home buyer's fact sheet to help with your efforts); and/or

c) *The person is paid to help with the dream.* A person wants to continue to receive compensation for providing assistance or advice that helps to build your dream (or a component of it).

People who have shares in your dream take responsibility for seeing it come to pass.

Community of Champions: Build a team to support your D.R.E.A.M.S. Who's championing your dreams? Your objective is to involve as many people as necessary to help make your dreams everything you want them to be AND everything they are meant to be. The more you are able to nurture quality relationships to help you champion your dreams, the better. These champions will help you achieve your dream as if it were their own.

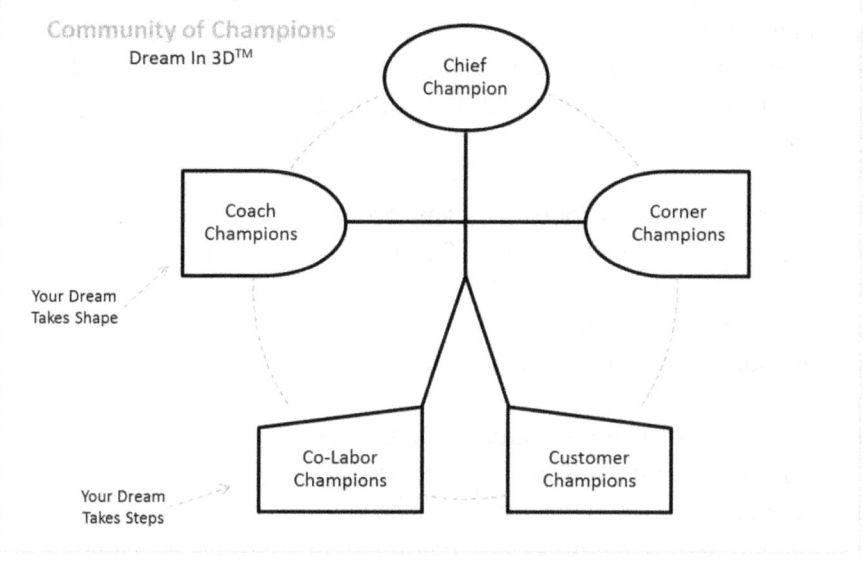

There are five roles that people will play as members of your community of champions:

- **Chief Champion** - the person most responsible for fulfilling the dream (you);

- **Corner Champions** - loved ones who are "in your corner" and support you personally as you pursue your dreams;

- **Coach Champions** - experienced role-models who offer trusted advice;

- **Co-Labor Champions** - skilled contributors who assist you with executing your plans; and

- **Consumer Champions** - people who benefit from, and value, your fulfilled dream.

Each role makes a unique contribution. The Chief Champion (you) leads all activities related to your dream. The Corner Champion and Coach Champion help to shape the dream by supporting your personal / professional development and helping you make decisions according what matters most to you and what's best for you. The Co-Labor champion and Customer Champion help you take steps necessary to achieve the dream by working with you to execute plans and offering feedback to enhance what you are doing.

The level of involvement for each champion role will differ depending upon the the specifics of a given dream. For one dream, one person may fulfill most, if not all, of the roles. Yet, for another dream, you may need hundreds of people. Either way, be sure to account for each Community of Champions role when working on your dreams.

Share your dream with a Community of Champions that will support you in making your vision a reality as well as helping you to expand your vision beyond your original concept (when necessary).

▶ Chief Champion

The Chief Champion is the author of the dream…which is you! You are the first, and leading, champion of your own dream.

There are a few things for you to remember as the Chief Champion:
- You are the only person responsible for the achievement of your dream.
- No one else owes you to assist with your dream.
- Expect no one to do for you more than you are willing to do for yourself.

Tips for being a Chief Champion:
- Complete Dream in 3D so you have a strong sense of your vision and the vehicles that will get you where you want to be.
- Take full ownership of your dream. "If it is to be, it's up to me."
- Schedule your D.R.E.A.M.S. first when planning your day / week / month.
- Take action towards your goals daily – no matter how big or small. Lead the momentum.

▶ Corner Champion

The corner champion is the person who loves you just as you are. The Corner Champion is more so concerned for you as a person than they are about the specific dream. Corner Champions are normally family members or friends who love you unconditionally and simply want to see you happy in life.

Corner Champions offer:
- Unconditional love (meaning, they love you as you are, for better or for worse);
- Truth that helps you make adjustments necessary to be a better person;
- Long-term support (meaning, they are in it with you for the long haul); and
- Perspectives that are based upon knowing the entire context of your life.
- Temporary participation in specific activities to help you fill-in the gaps on your team until a more permanent assistant comes along.

Tips for nurturing your Corner Champions:
- Corner Champions support your personal needs for love, motivation, and honest feedback. Focus on your personal needs and leverage Corner Champions to support your heart and you pursue your dreams.
- Corner Champions cannot read your mind, so you are responsible for expressing your needs.
- Corner Champions may or may not get directly involved in your dream fulfillment activities. Appreciate the love they offer to you as a person. Do not guilt them into taking on your projects.

Coach Champion

The Coach Champion is the person who models characteristics and/or accomplishes that you wish to emulate; or possesses some level of expertise or experiences due to which the person is able to offer insights and ideas that help you...and does so in a coaching/counselor/mentor-like manner. The coach, like the Corner Champion, is more so interested in you as a person than they are in getting directly involved in making the dream happen.

Coach Champions offer:
- A role model for you to have an idea of how to approach your dream;
- Guidance based upon their experiences - which saves you time and headaches;
- Valued advice for when making key decisions; and
- Big picture perspectives so that you do not get lost during your journey to your dream completion.

Tips for identifying and nurturing your Coach Champions:
- Let the person know how you view them and that you will be seeking his/her advice
- Select a coach based on character.
- Select a coach based on competence in a specific area related to your dream
- Select a coach based on completions

- select a coach based on comfort and the coach's communicated interest in you and your dream(s)
- Set clear goals for engaging a coach
- Maintain perspective that the coach help shape a dream but may not make it happen with you.
- Get comfortable with someone knowing your blindspots. You are not expected to know it all.
- Stick to facts as much as possible rather than allow emotion to cloud how you engage coach advice

Co-Labor Champion

The Co-Labor Champion is the person who is helping to work on your dream (or a specific aspect), directly. This person may be paid to render a service in interest of your dream and/or a person who is offering support as a peer, or otherwise, due to a shared interest in seeing the dream come to pass.

Co-Labor Champions can:
- Increase your progress
- Supplement your strengths and gaps in resources
- Expand your resource network
- Save you time by assisting with executing plans

Tips for identifying and nurturing Co-Labor Champions:
- Be clear on your goal and how the person will contribute
- Be clear on the win / win proposition
- Verify the character and competence
- Be clear with communication
- Delegate tasks but do not abdicate your role as the leader of your dream. You are still responsible for your own dream and the successful completion of plans.
- have a back up plan in case things do not work out
- If your co-laborer is also a loved-one (e.g. family or close friend), be extra clear on boundaries, timelines for ending parts of the project, and an agreed approach to managing conflict. The relationship comes first and Corner Champions are rare).. if the project is not working, just find someone else.

Customer Champion
A Customer Champion is a person who benefits from what your dream offers, once it's completed, and, therefore, offers support either by (a) making recommendations that help to further development of your offerings and/or, (b) spreading the word about your dream to other interested parties who would also like to experience it.

Customer Champions can:
- Confirm value of the completed dream
- Increase your motivation
- Offer helpful feedback
- Become your most enthusiastic champions
- Help make your offering bigger than you originally imagined

Considerations for Your Community of Champions
In addition to knowing the various types of champions, it is important to keep the following in mind:

- **Be the champion that you seek in others.** The best approach to quality relationships is to set your sights upon mutual fulfillment. When you approach relationships with the goal of figuring out how both parties can win, that approach increases possibilities for everyone. Creating value for others leads to more value for you. When you genuinely become a championing for others, more people will be excited to champion your dreams as well.
- **Champions are human.** Nurturing relationships is not an easy process. It requires patience as you work through communication and conflicts. Remember, even your best champion is human. You will likely be disappointed or discouraged by any person working with you, for one reason or another. Similarly, there are times when you will be a pain in someone else's neck also! This is a normal part of relationships. Maintain a patient posture and learn to work through the challenges of human imperfections.

My Community of Champions Profiler
This is brief survey is designed to gain initial insight about your approach to cultivating a Community of Champions. Using your best judgment, rate

yourself for each of the following statements. The rating scale is as follows:

- ☑ Place a check mark in the box for each statement that you do well.
- ☒ Place an "x" in the box for each statement that you do sometimes but know you need to do a little extra.
- ☐ Leave a box blank if you never do that item but need to start.

Category 1: Chief Champion
- ☐ I champion my own dreams 100%.
- ☐ I expect more from myself than I expect from others.
- ☐ I take full responsibility for completing my dreams.

Category 2: Corner Champion
- ☐ I share my dreams with my loved ones. I express my hope for their participation.
- ☐ I understand that love and support come in various forms and that my loved ones are not obligated participate in the specifics of my dream as proof of their love for me.
- ☐ I champion the dreams of my loved ones.

Category 3: Coach Champion
- ☐ I share my dreams with a mentor, coach, and/or role model.
- ☐ I attempt to implement the insights of my mentor/coach.
- ☐ I champion the dreams of others whom I mentor/coach.

Category 4: Co-Labor Champion
- ☐ I leverage the skills of others who help me fulfill dreams.
- ☐ I cultivate win/win relationships with those who help me.
- ☐ I champion the dreams of others by offering my strengths, skills, and support.

Category 5: Customer Champion
- ☐ I develop dreams that benefit others/customers.
- ☐ I invite customers (and others who benefit from my dream) to assist with improving my results.

☐ I champion the dreams of others by helping to spread the word about their work and/or giving helpful advice to improve offerings.

# of checks (☑) _____   # of x's (☒) _____   # of blanks (☐) _____

The more ☑'s you have, the more closely you are aligned with a balanced Community of Champions profile. If you do not have as many ☑'s as you would like, decide now to do what it takes to make all of the statements a part of your routine.

Next Steps
1. Review key concepts from this section

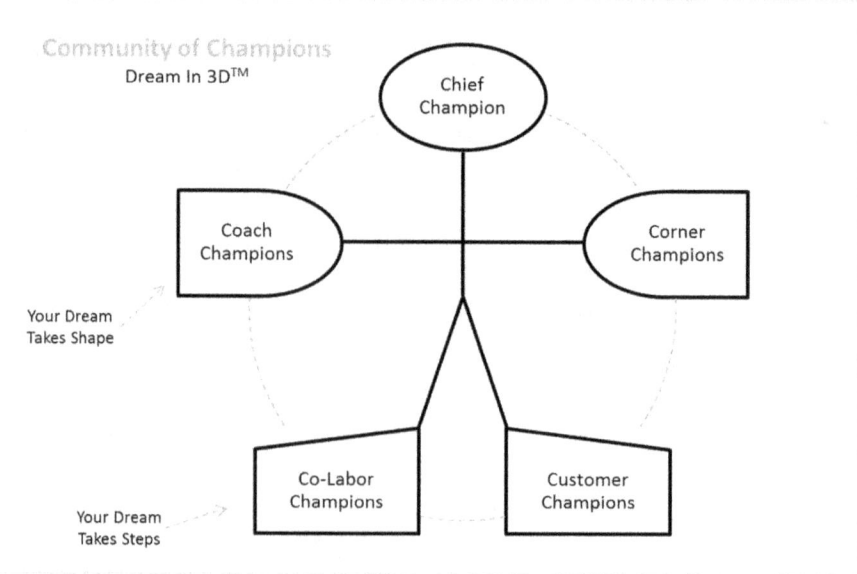

2. Reflect on your previous pursuit of goals.

- Who tends to help champion your dreams?

  _____
  _____
  _____

- Which champion roles do you enegage the most?

_____
_____
_____

- Which champions do you tend to engage least?

_____
_____
_____

- What do you stand to gain by fully engaging a community of champions in your dreams?

_____
_____
_____

3. Return to LIFE'S Legacy goal identified on pages 42 and 52. List your possible champions for that vision in the space provided below. Identify any category of champions that you are missing. Brainstorm possibilities for filling in those gaps.

   This is my Community of Champions. plan for the following goal:

   _____
   _____

   - Who is the Chief Champion of this goal?

   _____
   _____
   _____

   - List at least 3 Corner Champions who may support me as I pursue this goal.

   _____
   _____
   _____

- List at least 3 Coach Champions who may mentor me as I pursue this goal.

  _____
  _____
  _____

- List at least 3 Co-Labor Champions who may assist me with completing specific steps and tasks as I pursue this goal.

  _____
  _____
  _____

- List at least 3 Customer Champions who may confirm and/or spread the word about the completion of my dream. .

  _____
  _____
  _____

Introduction
EVOLUTION OF A DREAMER
Enjoy your life's journey by maintaining a balanced perspective.

Balanced Perspectives: Peace. Flow. Pace.

Pursuing your dreams is a very challenging job. While the processes outlined in this book (i.e. discover my purpose, develop my paths, distribute through people) are key strategies for achieving your goals, continued success is never as easy as 1-2-3 steps to the perfect life. It takes hard work and patience – especially during the times when it seems like you are making little-to-no progress. How you see, interpret, and leverage your experiences will greatly influence the quality of your follow-through and the fulfillment of your dreams.

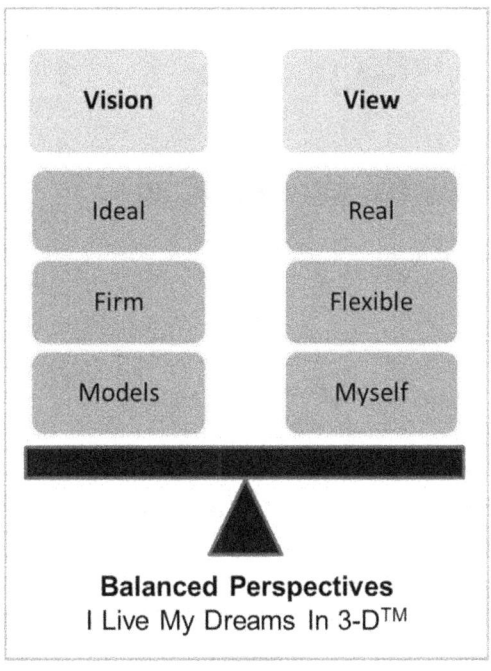

Balanced Perspectives
I Live My Dreams In 3-D™

Maintain a balanced perspective that creates harmony between your vision *(how you want things to be)* and your view *(how things are)*. The results will include the peace, flow, and pace necessary for your continued evolution as a successful dreamer.

Peace: Aspire for your wants. Appreciate your haves.

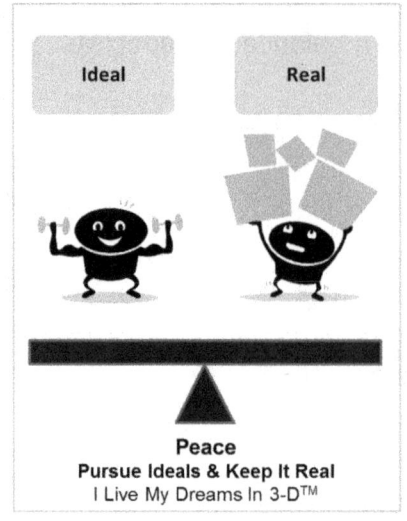

There is how you want things to be for your future, and then there is how things are in the present. You experience peace (inner contentment) when you appreciate your life as It is today and, at the same time, aspire to achieve the dreams that will lead to a better life tomorrow.

Balancing appreciation and aspiration is the key. When you get overly absorbed in your aspirations, you undervalue your present life. When you get overly absorbed in appreciation of your present life, you unvervalue the potential benefits of you progressing .

Flow: Be firm about where you are going and flexibile with how you get there.

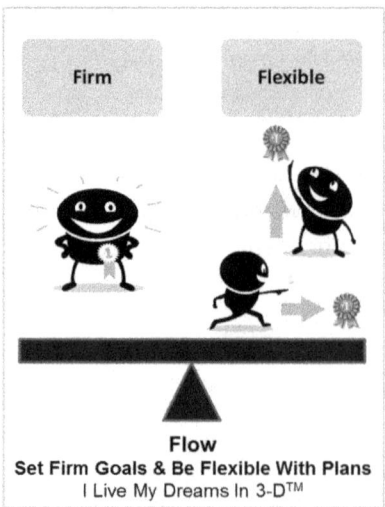

There is how you want things to go, and then there is how things actually will go. Sometimes your journey to your dreams will goes exactly as planned; many more times there will be unexpected and undersired twists and turns. Either way, you must stay in the flow. You know you are in the flow when you are firm about what you want, overall, but remain flexible about how your wants are fulfilled.

Again, balance is the key to living in a good flow. When you are too firm about how life goes, you limit your options and opportunities. When you are too flexible, you limit your progress due to lack of a defined path.

Pace: Use models as a guide as you continue to move in your own stride.

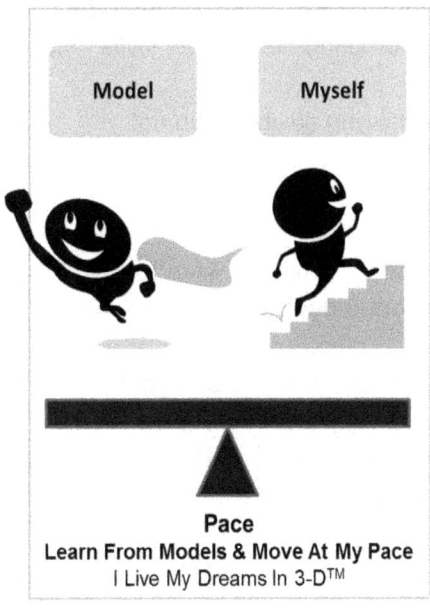

Pace
Learn From Models & Move At My Pace
I Live My Dreams In 3-D™

As you pursue your dreams, you will see models who reflect what you want to achieve. There is how your role models achieved their dreams, and then there is how you will achieve yours. Results will vary.

The goal is to move forward at a pace that is motivated by models but customized by your unique story. When you are too focused on models, you lose yourself. When you are too focused on yourself, you get lost in your comfort zone and lose the motivation to perform beyond your norm.

My Dreamer's Evolution Profile
This is a great time to consider your perspectives. Use the survey below as a guide for reflection. Read each statement. ☑ Place a check next to each statement that you do well. ☒ Place an "x" next to each statement that you do sometimes but know you need to improve. ☐ Leave a statement blank if it is an item that you do not do at present. Category 1: Peace ☐ I appreciate my life experience as it is today. ☐ I aspire to achieve dreams that will lead to a better life experience. ☐ I successfully balance my appreciation and aspirations; I do not emphasize one over the other.

Category 2: Flow
- ☐ I am firm about my goals. I set a target and pursue it through to completion.
- ☐ I am flexible about my how I achieve my goals. I remain open to alternatives, even when that means adopting new views, skills, and strategies.
- ☐ I successfully balance being firm and being flexible; I do not emphasize one over the other.

Category 3: Pace
- ☐ I identify (role) models with achievements similar to what I seek; I use them for motivation, making informed decisions, and avoiding uneeded mistakes.
- ☐ I embrace myself, what makes me unique, and I pursue goals in a mode of operation that best suits me.
- ☐ I successfully balance learning from (role) models and leaning on my own experiences; I do not emphasize one over the other.

# of checks (☑) _____   # of x's (☒) _____   # of blanks (☐) _____

Perspective 1
PEACE
Aspire for your wants. Appreciate your haves.

"We can never obtain peace in the outer world until we make peace with ourselves." - Dalai Lama

"I stop to smell the roses and simultaneously seed a new garden" – Brian Jones

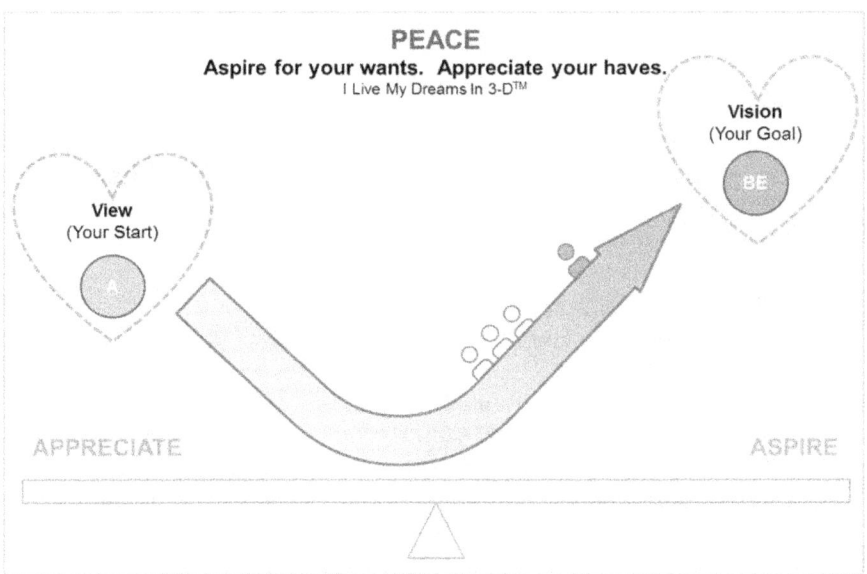

Peace is the inner contentment that you experience when there is harmony between your ideals *(i.e. how you want things to be)* and your reality *(i.e. how things are)*. Maintaining peace is a matter of enjoying life as it is in reality (appreciation) while simultaneously pursuing life as it is in your dream (aspiration).

Appreciation is when you recognize the quality, value, significance, and/or magnitude of your present circumstances, relationships, possessions, and progress in life. When you have a deep appreciation for life, you:

- Enjoy life in the present, rather than living a life of continual preparation for some future circumstance where you will finally

be happy (a future state that never seems to materialize because you never appreciate what you have achieved).
- Gain confidence as you recognize what is possible based upon your progress to date as well as the resources you have at your disposal.
- Fuel your faith and hope because you have experienced some of the fruit of your labor and have tasted enough success to hunger for more progress.
- Experience more happiness about your life (e.g. health and wellness, relationships, career, etc) as you intentionally count and celebrate your blessings.

Appreciation of your life, as it is today, is the beginning of your peace. Be grateful. Be thankful. This is the foundation of inner contentment and peace of mind.

Aspiration is a hope or ambition of achieving a specific goal, milestone, and/or vision. Simply put, an anspiration is an ideal, or a dream, that you want to make a reality. When you have aspirations in life, you:

- Enjoy a clarity of purpose.
- Have an objective towards which to apply all of your strengths, skills, and resources.
- Engage various life adventures and challenges that test and confirm your character and competence; and it often leads to new opportunities for growth and development.
- Have a fresh reason to wake up in the morning even if your aspiration is simply to sustain the peace that you enjoyed yesterday.

Aspirations are powerful motivators. There is an inner peace that comes with having a clear vision for your desired progress and knowing that you will take steps to make your dream a reality in the midst of any challenges that may arise. The peace is a result of seeing that you can positively influence your life circumstances rather than just being helplessly impacted by whatever life presents you.

When you balance your appreciation and aspiration, you benefit in many ways.

- You get to enjoy (be excited) about your past, present, and future...all at the same. This is the ultimate peace.
- You live life with poise - freedom from affectation or embarrassment; composure. You live a balanced life that is void

of apathy (lack of aspirations) and anxiousness (lack of appreciation). This is a peaceful path.
- You enjoy a confidence about your past and present as well as your pursuits.
- You will lead a life of consistent satisfaction, knowing that your time has been, and will continue to be, put to great use.

This ultimately adds up to a life of peace.

When you get overly absorbed in your aspirations, you undervalue your present life.
Do you tend to focus too much on your aspirations (so much so that you have very little appreciation for your present circumstances)? Here are common characteristics of a person who focuses too much upon aspirations for the future:

- You do not have time to enjoy life right now. You will enjoy life only when you finally achieve perfection.
- You feel guilty if you are not actively working towards my goals 24 hours a day, 7 days a week. Relaxing is considered to be a waste of time.
- You look at the success of others in order to determine the standards for your own achievements. You often compare myself to others, and you never seem to be able to "keep up with the Joneses."

If you find that this is you, try the following:

1. **Make friends with a person who appreciates and celebrates life…often**. Engage a Corner Champion and / or a Coach Champion who is well known for enjoying life. Schedule at least one time a week during which you will connect with this person in order to relax, discuss areas of your life for which you are thankful, highlight your progress with various endeavors and projects, and, most importantly, to have fun. Allow the person to recommend the environments that best suit a celebratory conversation. These sessions will help you better appreciate your life.
2. **Count your blessings and name them – one by one**. Do the following:

    - Each morning, jot down at least five reasons for which you are thankful for your life. Repeat this activity before bed.

- Each time you are about to begin a project, list out at least five reasons why it can work out and five times when you set a goal, took on the challenge, and achieved success.
- Each time you find yourself about to complain to someone about a situation in life, begin the conversation with at least three things you appreciate. For a bonus, share something you are grateful for about the situation you are intending to now complain about.

These types of exercises will help you develop the habit of appreciating your life (at present) as you continue to work towards fulfilling your aspirations.

When you get overly absorbed in appreciation of your present life, you unvervalue the potential benefits of you progressing.
Do you tend to focus too much on appreciating life as-is (so much so that you that you are not engaged in any healthy growth and development activities)? Here are common characteristics of a person who focuses too much upon present circumstances:

- You shift from contentment (i.e. a state of happiness and satisfaction) to becoming complacent (contented to the point where you are unconcerned with progress or you have uncritical satisfaction with yourself or your achievements).
- You have a pattern of "resting on your laurels" - which means that you are banking on your past achievements to automatically carry you into the future without any additional effort on your part.
- You overly promote your satisfaction with a present situation as a tactic to avoid acknowledging and addressing the aspects you are putting up with - much to your dissatisfaction. This typically occurs when you are not certain that you have what it takes to create a more desireable situation and/or you are not certain that the effort required for change will be worth it when all is said and done.

Overly appreciating a a present situation / circumstance can also be a procrastination tactic to avoid:

- The work of figuring out your purpose and/or working on your plan and/or following through on activities and/or taking a step that causes great nervousness;
- The frustration and pain that sometimes accompanies trying to figure out how you will actually go about achieving your goal.

You know where you want to go, but you do not see how you are going to get there;
- The potential embarrassment of putting your dream out there and things not working out as planned; and/or
- Anything else that represents pain associated with progress.

If you find that this is you, try the following:

1. **Make friends with a goal-oriented person**. Recruit a Corner Champion and/or Coach Champion who has a genuine interest in helping you to clarify and achieve your dreams. This person will help surface and address any apathy. The goal is to be certain that you are not minimizing your goals in the interests of a false sense of peace, avoiding fears or challenges for which you have no current answer, and/or anything else that would keep you from fulfilling your dreams. Meet with this person at least once a week. Use the time to discuss your your current place in life (View) as compared to where you want to be (Vision). If you find that there is a gap between your View and your Vision, discuss doable ideas for closing that gap. As a result of the sessions, you will (a) confirm that you are where you want to be; or (b) clarify what you really want and challenge you to take steps towards progress.

2. **Reflect upon your goals**. Review the exercises in the "Discover My Purpose" and "Develop My Paths" sections of this book on a daily basis. Pay special attention to your answers related to your desired LIFE'S Legacy as well as the steps you listed as part of achieving your D.R.E.A.M.S. These exercises will help inspire you to reengage your vision for your life.

Perspective 2
FLOW

Be firm about where you are going and flexible with how you get there.

"Dwell as near as possible to the channel in which your life flows."
- Henry David Thoreau

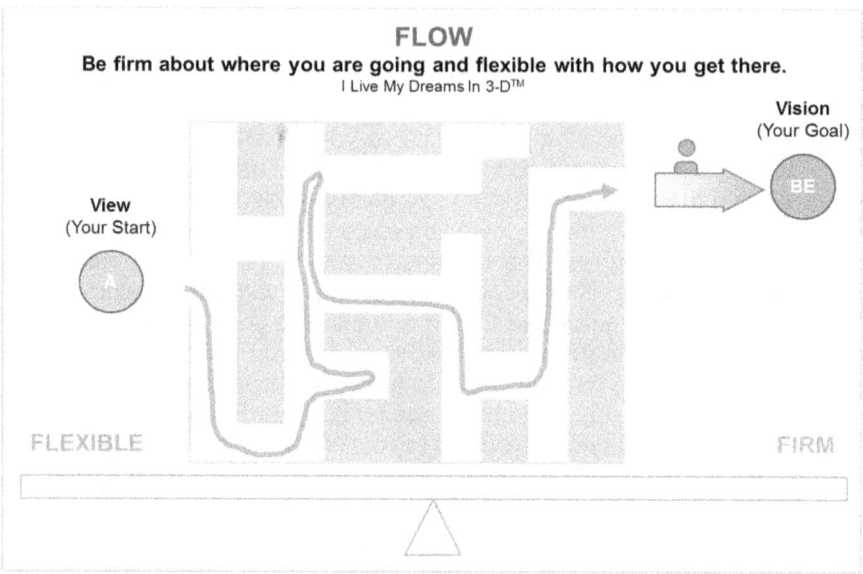

You will succeed to the extent that you are able to go with the flow. "Flow" is when you progress steadily towards a goal in a continuous manner that is unbroken by changes in your context, course, or circumstances. Flow occurs when there is harmony between your purposed destination and the various paths you may take in order to get there. Being firm about what you want to achieve, while simultaneously being flexible about your courses of action, is the key to enjoying your life's flow.

Being firm (i.e. definite, certain, unwavering) about where you are headed is vital any dream pursuit. Focusing intensely upon a given purpose, and being unwavering in your mission, will yield optimal results. A famous Bible quote reads, "A double-minded man is unstable in all his ways." Being stable, strong, and sure leads to a sense of confidence in oneself, and it attracts the trust of others. Being firm about where you are headed in life provides a solid foundation upon which you can build your dreams.

Life is dynamic. Flexibility is a must when living in a world of constant change. This means being (a) capable of bending without breaking, and (b) able to easily modify your approach to respond to altered circumstances or conditions. There's a saying that goes, "The only thing constant in this world is change." Your ability to adapt to change, while maintaining the core characteristics that make you who you are, is a key to success.

Be firm about where you are going, while being flexible about how you get there.
Cultivate harmony between where you are going (your purpose) and how you get there (your paths). As you do so, you will:

- Follow through on more opportunities because you are open to more options for completing your specific goal.
- Save time and energy by simply making adjustments along the way to your destination rather than always having to start over when things change.
- Plan better by considering your alternatives prior to, and during, your journey.
- Become a results oriented person who is able to win by any means (rather than needing to stick to one approach).

You will experience some delays, detours, distractions, difficulties, and "didn't know that would happen" moments as you pursue your dreams. The key is not to be deterred; you will just approach it another way.

Marry your purpose. Divorce yourself from the path. In other words, do not get caught up in having to do it one way. Focus more on experiencing your fulfillment by whatever means are best for you within your context at that time.

When you are too firm, you limit your options and opportunities.
Are you too firm about your approach? Here are common characteristics of a person who is too firm:
- ☐ You tend to have "all or nothing" thinking. You try one plan. You assume it is the only way to go. If it does not work, you stop all attempts to pursue your dream.
- ☐ You have chosen one way of approaching life. You avoid making changes and adjustments.
- ☐ You are easily annoyed by new ideas and recommendations that require you try something new.

When you are too firm, everything is about staying committed to one idea, one path, or one opportunity as compared to being open to alternatives for reaching your goal.

If you find that this is you, try the following:

1. **Make friends with an opportunist.** Find a Corner Champion, or Coach Champion, who is known for being adventurous, enterprising, innovative, and open for trying new experiences and ways of doing things. Meet with this person weekly to share about your respective endeavors. Commit to sharing your purpose and proposed course of action with this person <u>before</u> you start on your next project. Allow the person to offer you at least 2-3 alternatives for you to consider. This will challenge you at first because: (a) you were ready to move forward and already had a plan; and, (b) while you may like the new ideas, most likely they will be outside of your comfort zone, or else you would have thought of them yourself. Follow-through on at least one new suggestion each month. This will be good for you as it will help you to be more creative and open to the flow.

2. **Commit to asking yourself the following every time that you have a goal you are pursuing:**

    - What are at least three ways that you can achieve your goal (list your chosen approach along with two good alternatives)?

    - What resources will I need access to in order to take advantage of these different options?

    - Who are some people/models that have tried these different options? What did they do?

These steps will help you to be less rigid about your plan and more open to opportunities should you need an alternative or detour.

When you are too flexible, you get lost in too many options and opportunities (so much so that you do not make significant progress).
Are you too flexible? Here are common characteristics of a person who is too flexible:
- ☐ You are addicted to brainstorming.
- ☐ You collect new ideas but never truly commit to one long enough to realize its full potential.

☐ You have many incomplete projects. You start a new project with intensity. Then you lose enthusiasm and begin another project. This cyle repeats often.

There's absolutely nothing wrong with having new ideas. However, if you continue to entertain new ideas when you have not completed enough of your original plan to see results and to make a true assessment of how it worked (or not), you will not experience consistent progress.

If you find that this is you, you'll want to do one of the following :

1. **Make friends with a decisive, doer**. Recruit a Corner Champion, or Coach Champion, who is a decision-maker known for starting and completing projects. This person will be the type to limit ideas to 2-3 top options, make a decision on the best one for the moment, and move forward without mentally rehearsing what potentially could have happened with the other opportunities. This person quickly assesses the pros and cons of the options presented, and this person moves forward with the confidence that the option selected was the best one for the moment. Undistracted by externalities, this person is the type to complete the decided course-of-action enough to measure the true results BEFORE entertaining new ideas. Meet with this person at least once a week. Share your ideas. Allow this person to help you prioritize and commit to a course of action to complete. This person will confirm the completion of your project before you move on to something new. This will help you move forward and stick to a plan long enough for you to reap the rewards of your actions or are able to truly say you tried it and did not get the results (and, therefore, can move onto with the next idea).

2. **Set boundaries for yourself**. The next time you plan, only allow for 2-3 options, select an option, and work-it to completion before allowing yourself to look at any new ideas. Do what you must to keep yourself from distractions. Turn off the TV. Do not read any additional information in books or online. Do not entertain new ideas from your (codependent) associates ☺. Commit to a plan and excute it fully.

Perspective 3
PACE
Use Models As A Guide. Move Forward In Your Own Stride.

But it's for every [person] to decide his own pace, and the pace varies with the [person] and the work.
- Donna Tartt

"Why should we be in such desperate haste to succeed, and in such desperate enterprises? If a man loses pace with his companions, perhaps it is because he hears a different drummer. Let him step to the music in which he hears, however measured, or far away."
- Henry David Thoreau

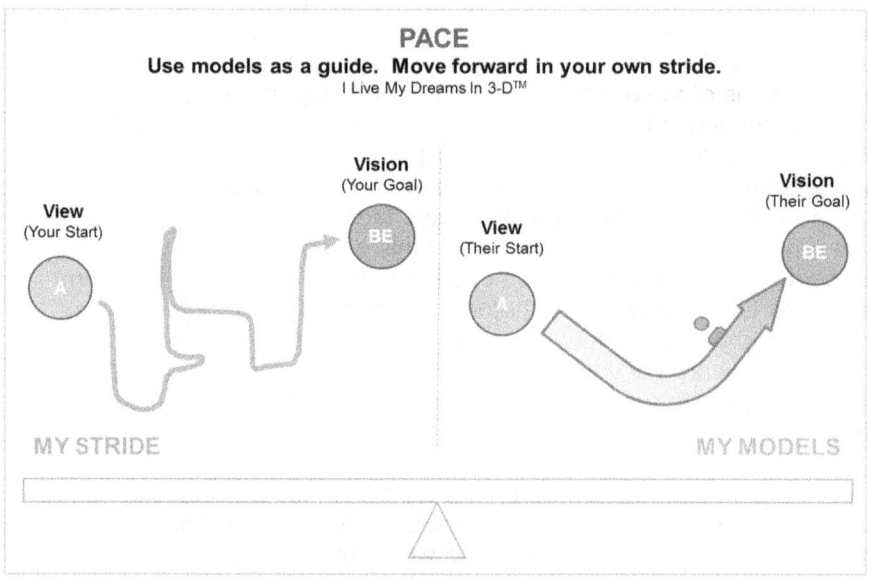

Pace is the rate of speed at which you progress towards a goal. Your optimum pace occurs when there is harmony between the influence of your (role) models and the modes of operation that work best for you. The key to pace is to use models for helpful information and motivation and then move forwards based upon your strengths and your unique circumstances.

A model is a person (or an organization) that performs and produces results in a way that you (and others) consider to be ideal. A model typically: (a) shows you how to achieve a particular result (skill power), and/or (b) motivates you to pursue a particular result (will power). A model also helps you to figure out what you want to do (vision). There are times when you are trying to figure out what it is that you want to do and then you see a model that is getting results that resonate with you to the point that you say, "Ah ha! There it is! THAT is what I want to achieve."

It typically follows that you attempt to imitate or replicate the steps taken by the model. In some cases, it works according to plan. In most cases, you will not experience the exact same results due to differences between you and that model.

It is important for you to understand self – meaning, the essential qualities that distinguishes you from others. There are characteristics that make you uniquely you: how you perceive, perform, relate to people, and produce as an individual. Together, those characteristics make up your identity. It is important to be clear about your identity. The more you are clear about who you are, the better you will be able to compare yourself to models. There will be similarities and differences between yourself and your models. A proper comparison will be helpful in allowing you to use the model as a guide, while you continue to move forward in a stride that fits your true self.

When you use models as guides, while moving in your stride, you will:
- Equally appreciate the value of your models and your self worth.
- Appreciate the performance and production of the model, while setting realistic expectations for yourself based on your unique context.
- Enjoy more peace and serenity as you adjust your perception of models from being the standards to being examples. Therefore, your goal is not to become the model, but rather to learn from the model in order to achieve your vision at a pace that is true to your self.

When you focus too much on models, you lose yourself.
Do you tend to focus too much on models? Here are common characteristics of a person who focuses too much upon models:
- ☐ You want to be just like the model.
- ☐ You assume something is wrong with you when you take the same approach as the model but your results are not similar to the model.
- ☐ In your eyes, there is no other way the way of the model. You treat the model as the only standard.

There's a difference between appreciating a model and idolizing a model. When you appreciate the model, you admire and applaud what the model has done. You look for ways to incorporate some of the characteristics of the model that would benefit you. When you idolize the model, you view the model as THE way it always should be done. You attempt to emulate the model exactly. In some cases, you may clone the model. In many cases, however, you results will vary.

Typically, there are unique characteristics of the model that influenced how the model performed and produced results. In addition, there is usually more than meets the eye. Unless you were part of the model's journey, you are normally missing certain details and factors that were part of the process. When you are too focused upon the model as being the only standard, you tend to miss those subtle distinctions between yourself and the model and, therefore, have extreme expectations for yourself to produce in the same exact manner as the model.

If you find that you focus too much on models, try the following:

1. **Make friends with a trendsetter**. Recruit a Corner Champion, or a Coach Champion, who is known for being an independent thinker. This person will be characterized by self-confidence and a desire to pursue new ideals and create models that express a unique vision and mission. As you are gathering information on the models that you seek to replicate, share your ideas with this person and allow them to help you customize the models, and related courses of action, to make fit your vision.

2. **Commit to identify at least five similarities and five differences between yourself and the model that you are seeking to replicate**. Thoroughly research characteristics and contextual factors that influence both performance and productivity. Ask yourself how the similarities and differences may result in different outcomes between yourself and the model.   Reflect upon what makes you unique and how that will result in an equally valuable model as you maximize your options and opportunities.

When you focus too much upon your own mode of operations, you get lost in yourself.
Do you tend to get lost in yourself? Here are characteristics of a person who focuses too much upon self:
- You look at yourself as the sole standard. You do not recognize any other models as being valid.
- You believe that your vision and circumstances are so unique that there is no other model for you to consider.

The world, as you see it, only includes what you choose to see and how you see it (otherwise referred to as your world view or mental model). While in some cases this does lead to innovation (in that you are not being overly influenced by what is going on out in the world), in many cases it leads to repeating mistakes that have already been committed by the models AND / OR missing out on key information that would help you progress in a better manner.

In addition, when you are too focused upon self, you tend to only move at a pace that is based upon your current story, strengths, skills, and sources of support. You miss out on would have been possible for you had you looked to a few models to help you improve your approach.

If you find that this is you, try one of the following:

1. **Make friends with a person who watches and follows trends**. Recruit a Corner Champion, or Coach Champion, who is known for keeping up with trends and lessons shared by others. This person will be the type who can produce at least five various models for the goals that you have in mind. This person will be able to explain the similarities and differences between yourself and the models. Commit to sharing your thoughts with this person prior to moving forward with your plans so that this champion can help inform you of any pre-existing models that you should consider as you make decisions about your course of action.

2. **Commit to borrowing ideas from models**. Commit to researching at least three models for each idea that you have. Since you are likely to focus on how different you are, list at least five similarities between yourself and the models that you select. This will help you give more credibility to the models and, therefore, be able to learn more from the models. List at least one takeaway from each model – i.e. a principle or practice that you can leverage for your own idea.

A Final Thought
DREAM. REALITY. SAME THING.

I am fueled by the belief that the life of your dreams can be your reality. This belief inspired "I Live My Dreams In 3-D" and other endeavors I've pursued over the years.

It would be dishonest for me to say that my life matches the exact vision that I have in mind for myself and my community. I still have a ways to go to completely fulfill my LIFE'S Legacy. However, the belief that I can influence the achievement of my dreams is what wakes me up in the morning. It gives me life. It ignites my faith. It motivates me to find ways to succeed even when I am overwhelmed by internal and external obstacles. It inspires me to support the dreams of my family, friends, students, clients, and others who are interested in seeing their visions come to life.

Rembember, **making your dreams a reality is about the processes you repeat (discover, develop, distribute) and the perspectives you rehearse (peace, flow, pace).** Above all, it begins with the belief that fulfilling your vision is possible and then following-through with the activities that will propel you towards your goals. When you stop and reflect upon your desired LIFE'S Legacy, you will agree that your dreams are more than worth the daily effort!

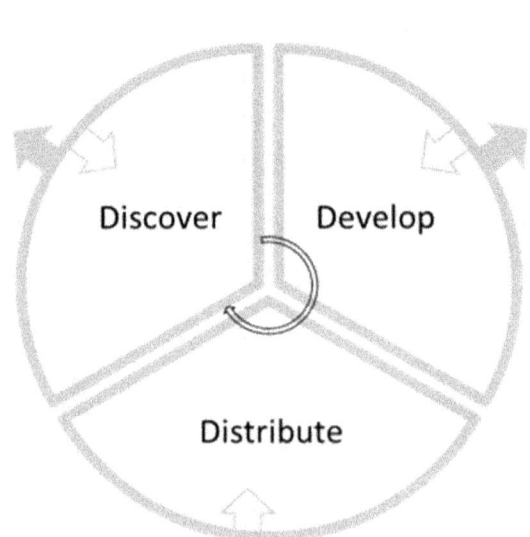

www.ingramcontent.com/pod-product-compliance
Lightning Source LLC
Chambersburg PA
CBHW060408050426
42449CB00009B/1936